Consumption and Public Life

The series will be a channel and focus for some of the most interesting recent work on consumption, establishing innovative approaches and a new research agenda. New approaches and public debates around consumption in modern societies will be pursued within media, politics, ethics, sociology, economics, management and cultural studies.

Owen Abbott • Vanessa May
Sophie Woodward • Robert Meckin
Leah Gilman

Masking in the Pandemic

Materiality, Interaction, and Moral Practice

palgrave
macmillan

Owen Abbott
School of Social Sciences
Cardiff University
Cardiff, UK

Vanessa May
Department of Sociology
University of Manchester
Manchester, UK

Sophie Woodward
Department of Sociology
University of Manchester
Manchester, UK

Robert Meckin
School of Social Sciences
University of Manchester
Manchester, UK

Leah Gilman
Centre for Social Ethics and Policy
University of Manchester
Manchester, UK

ISSN 2947-8227 ISSN 2947-8235 (electronic)
Consumption and Public Life
ISBN 978-3-031-45780-7 ISBN 978-3-031-45781-4 (eBook)
https://doi.org/10.1007/978-3-031-45781-4

This Palgrave Macmillan imprint is published by the registered company Springer Nature Switzerland AG.
The registered company address is: Gewerbestrasse 11, 6330 Cham, Switzerland

Paper in this product is recyclable.

Acknowledgements

This book began life as an informal writing group for members of the Morgan Centre for Research into Everyday Lives at the start of the Covid-19 pandemic in the spring of 2020. We met online to share our observations and sociological puzzlings on how to make sense of a social world that was changing before our eyes. Although the writing group did not start out specifically focusing on masks, much of the ethos and approach of the initial writing group informed the book on masking that we have developed. We would therefore like to thank those members of the Morgan Centre for Research into Everyday Lives—of which we are all members—who participated in the writing and discussion group for their time, thoughts, and sociological wonderings. We would like to acknowledge the specific contribution of Jennifer Mason, who was a key part of the writing group in its early stages. Jennifer also provided insightful feedback on early ideas for developing our discussions and observations about masking into a formalised text. We would also like to acknowledge David Morgan, after whom the Morgan Centre is named. David was a keen participant in the writing group at the start of the pandemic, but sadly died in June 2020. The enormity of David's sociological legacy was matched by how generous he was with his time and thoughts. He developed a wonderful observational sociological approach across his work, and this approach has inspired the way we have written this book. More broadly, the Morgan Centre has been instrumental in providing a space for us to develop as sociologists, offering us all an academic home for thinking through everyday lives from a multitude of perspectives.

Owen Abbott would also like to acknowledge the funding of the Leverhulme Trust, which has made work on this book possible.

Contents

About the Authors

Owen Abbott Owen's research focuses on moral practices and morality in interaction. He has published articles on moral theory and moral practices, and his book *The Self, Relational Sociology, and Morality in Practice* won the British Sociological Association's Philip Abrams prize for best first sole authored book in sociology, 2020. His next book, *Social Theorists of Morality*, will be published in 2024 by Palgrave. He is currently undertaking a Leverhulme early career research fellowship, investigating forgiveness in personal relationships.

Vanessa May Vanessa is Professor and Head of Sociology at the University of Manchester, UK. Her research interests include the self, belonging, temporality, ageing, family relationships, and qualitative methods. Vanessa has published in a number of journals including *Sociology*, *Sociological Review*, *Time & Society*, and *British Journal of Sociology*. She is the author of *Connecting Self to Society: Belonging in a Changing World* (Palgrave Macmillan) and co-editor of *Sociology of Personal Life* (2nd edition, Red Globe).

Sophie Woodward Sophie is a Professor of Sociology at the Morgan Centre and Co-Director of the Morgan Centre for research into everyday lives at the University of Manchester. She is the author of five books on feminism, fashion, material culture and methods, the two most recent books are *Material Methods* (Sage, 2019) and *Birth and Death* (Routledge, 2019). She has an ongoing interest in creative methods and is currently writing a book on Dormant Things—people things keep but are no longer use—to think about dormancy as a phase in the lives of things.

Robert Meckin Robert's research focuses on methods of scientific knowledge production, particularly in biotechnology, health, and social science, and on processes of engagement, collaboration, and interdisciplinarity. He has published in *Sociology; Science, Technology, and Human Values;* and *Research Policy*. He is affiliated with the National Centre for Research Methods where he has co-authored reports about how researchers adapted methodologies during the Covid-19 pandemic and published the co-edited collection *Investigative Methods* (NCRM, 2022).

Leah Gilman Leah's research explores family and personal relationships in the context of social, technological, and regulatory change. She is currently leading a Wellcome Trust-funded study, exploring informal donor conception practices in the digital age. Leah's work is published in a number of academic journals and she is co-author of *Donors: Curious Connections in Donor Conception*, published in 2022 with Emerald Publishing.

CHAPTER 1

Introduction: Masks in the Pandemic, Masks in Everyday Life

Abstract This book is about the social significance of face masks and everyday social practice during the Covid-19 pandemic. As a material, medicalised object worn (or not) on one's face as a barrier to infection, the face mask became one of the most tangible ways in which the immense social changes wrought by the Covid-19 pandemic were made visible. Compared to other Covid-related measures, such as vaccines or often ambiguous rules on social distancing, the material visibility of face masks afforded them a unique significance to facilitating, hampering, and judging interactions during the height of the pandemic. This led not just to the implementation of formalised rules, but also to the rapid and seemingly spontaneous proliferation of new norms of how social situations were conducted and appraised. Tied as they were (and are) to the protection of life and health on the one hand and political imposition on the other, masks also quickly became imbued with moral meaning, becoming at once an object of responsibility, a 'symbol of care' towards others, and a medium of sociopolitical contestation. In a remarkably short time of profound social upheaval, masks moved from being for many (especially in Western contexts) an uncomfortable object of novelty, to being a mundane possession used in conjunction with everyday habits that was interwoven with symbolic meaning and expectations of social conduct.

O. Abbott et al., *Masking in the Pandemic*, Consumption and Public Life, https://doi.org/10.1007/978-3-031-45781-4_1

Keywords Masks • Everyday life • Interaction • Materiality • Morality • Facet methodology • Relational

This book is about the social significance of face masks and everyday social practice during the Covid-19 pandemic. As a material, medicalised object worn (or not) on one's face as a barrier to infection, the face mask became one of the most tangible ways in which the immense social changes wrought by the Covid-19 pandemic were made visible. Compared to other Covid-related measures, such as vaccines or often ambiguous rules on social distancing, the material visibility of face masks afforded them a unique significance to facilitating, hampering, and judging interactions during the height of the pandemic. This led not just to the implementation of formalised rules, but also to the rapid and seemingly spontaneous proliferation of new norms of how social situations were conducted and appraised. Tied as they were (and are) to the protection of life and health on the one hand and political imposition on the other, masks also quickly became imbued with moral meaning, becoming at once an object of responsibility, a 'symbol of care' towards others, and a medium of socio-political contestation (Lupton et al., 2021, p. xiii; Tateo, 2021). In a remarkably short time of profound social upheaval, masks moved from being for many (especially in Western contexts) an uncomfortable object of novelty, to being a mundane possession used in conjunction with everyday habits that was interwoven with symbolic meaning and expectations of social conduct.

The sudden global ubiquity of the face mask, its association with the threat of the virus, and its relationship with immense changes to pandemic sociality meant the mask 'has become the key symbol of the COVID crisis' (Lupton et al., 2021, p. 2). In this book, we attempt to explore the rapid and emergent changes in social life associated with the face mask during the pandemic. This book thus responds to Inglis and Almila's (2020, pp. 252, 255) call for sociologists to explore 'in new and deeper ways the many facets of Covid-19-related masking' and to 'examine the unfolding transformations' that masking gave rise to. In essence, this is a book about these unfolding (social) transformations, as viewed through the lens of masking practices.

We intend this book to offer a record of everyday experiences of masking during the height of the Covid-19 pandemic, which we hope gives the book a general appeal beyond specialist academic audiences. For academic audiences, this book firstly contributes to sociological understandings of the pandemic and facemasks, but also to general sociological accounts of interactional practice, materiality, morality, social and technical discourse, and the entwinement thereof. The nature of the book also means it is of interest to a variety of non-sociological audiences interested in masking, pandemic responses, and public health more broadly.

The Development of Masking in the UK Context

Masking in the Pandemic is written by academics based in the UK and will consequently focus primarily on the UK context. However, the rapid introduction of masking during the pandemic was a global phenomenon, meaning that our arguments throughout the book will draw on research into experiences of masking from across the world (e.g. Qian & Fuller, 2020; Chang et al., 2021; Dillard et al., 2021; Goyes et al., 2022). In contrast to East Asian contexts, face masks hardly featured in public settings in the UK prior to the pandemic (Chang et al., 2021; Qiaoan, 2020). The introduction of masking in the UK and similar contexts thus affords insight into the emergence of a new social practice, which developed with a rapidity necessitated by the circumstances of the pandemic. Yet the introduction of masking in the UK was somewhat more disjointed and contested than in other comparable nations (The Royal Society, 2020). Here we briefly set out the ways in which the implementation of masking and its comparatively early decline were unique to the UK, leading to specific uncertainties and contestations that are discussed throughout the book.

This book began to develop in the first half of 2020, a period of time during which the status of masks changed considerably. In the space of a few months, masking in the UK went from being almost non-existent in public to becoming widespread, both before and after the UK government mandated masking in most enclosed public spaces between July and August 2020. In the remainder of 2020 and throughout 2021, the face mask was no longer a novelty, but a fairly mundane object to be carried about our person 'alongside other mundane objects such as house keys and wallets' (Lupton et al., 2021, p. 33). We focus on the period between early 2020, when the pandemic began to take hold in the UK and discourses and practices around masking began to emerge, and early 2022, when masking rates began to decline rapidly after briefly re-introduced masking mandates were rescinded (YouGov, 2022). Throughout this period, the speed and scale of the introduction of masking in public settings produced substantial changes in social practice. We argue that these historically brief but sizable changes provide sociologists with a unique lens through which to theorise the nature of material, interactional, and moral practices in general. Indeed, whereas norms and practices tend to develop gradually, the rapidity of the introduction of masking, the widescale uptake of the practice in public (at least at the start of the pandemic), and the material visibility of masking affords a degree of observability to the development of masking practices.

Masking in public proliferated rapidly across the globe in the first half of 2020 as face masks came to be identified as a vital measure in reducing the profound risk posed by the novel SARS-CoV-2 virus (Smith, 2020; The Royal Society, 2020). Yet the UK context was somewhat particular in how faltering it was in its movement towards masking recommendations and mandates. Across the world, initial pandemic responses were framed by uncertainty. At the early stages of the pandemic, how the virus was primarily transmitted was not fully understood (Martin et al., 2020). The effectiveness of masks was also not at all clear, and indeed was initially doubted. For example, a World Health Organization (WHO) Interim Guidance document on face masks from 6 April 2020 stated 'there is currently no evidence that wearing a mask (whether medical or other types) by healthy persons in the wider community setting, including universal community masking, can prevent them from infection with respiratory viruses, including COVID-19' (World Health Organization, 2020b). Even once the efficacy of masks had become well evidenced and recommended by the WHO (World Health Organization, 2020a), uncertainties remained regarding who was protected by masks (the wearer, other people, or both) and whether masks were necessary outdoors as well as in doors (The Royal Society, 2020). In the UK and elsewhere, the use of scarves was seen as an alternative amongst uncertainties about how much the material of masks mattered (Lam et al., 2020). Debates on all these issues were vociferous and subject to rapid transformation as new evidence was sought and collated (Greenhalgh, 2020; Martin et al., 2020).

Governments and scientific advisors across the world had to contend with this uncertainty as a perennial feature of the Covid-19 pandemic. Throughout March and April 2020, the position of UK government officials and scientists was that evidence of the effectiveness of masking at preventing the spread of Covid-19 was mixed at best. Official advice from SAGE (the Scientific Advisory Group for Emergencies which liaised with the UK government throughout the pandemic) on the effectiveness of masking aligned with the early position given by the WHO (above):

namely that there was little evidence that masking was effective against the spread of Covid-19 (Reuters, 2020). Indeed, UK policymakers actively discouraged masking at the start of the pandemic. Concerns were expressed that members of the public would use up stocks of Personal Protective Equipment (PPE), which were then in short supply in the health service and in care homes (BBC News, 2020). Scientific advisors also suggested that because the efficacy of masking remained unclear, the wearing of face masks could impart a false sense of security, leading to other measures, such as social distancing, being ignored (The Independent, 2020). There were apprehensions (which turned out to be ill-founded) that the UK population would struggle to adopt masking, having had no prior history of the practice (The Royal Society, 2020). Indeed, it was only after an evidence review meeting on 21 April 2020 that SAGE began to change its guidance, at around the same time that the WHO revised their position in light of new evidence of the effectiveness of masks (GOV.UK, 2020; World Health Organization, 2020a).

Nevertheless, once the efficacy of masking was well-established, the implementation of masking mandates in the UK was slower and more disjointed than many similar nations. By the time it was decided that masking mandates should be introduced in England in July 2020, 120 countries (including Scotland and Ireland) had already implemented such policies (Blackburn, 2020). Delays in the introduction of masking mandates in England drew condemnation from various expert groups, including The Royal Society (2020) and the British Medical Association (BMA), with the latter chastising the government for its decision to leave an 11-day gap between the approval of masking mandates (on 13 July 2020) and the implementation of the rules in England (on 24 July 2020) (Blackburn, 2020). Indeed, the uptake of mask wearing in public was initially lower in the UK than other nations in Western Europe, which seems to be connected to conflicting political messaging about their necessity and effectiveness (Beaver & Skinner, 2020).

The uptake in masking did grow considerably once masking became mandated rather than just recommended, rising from 38% of people saying they had worn a face mask in a public place in the last 7 days[1] to 69% a week after the mandate was introduced (YouGov, 2022). Masking rates then remained over 70% in the UK until the masking mandate was first

[1] Note the framing of this question precludes those who have not been in a public place in the last 7 days.

lifted in England on 19 July 2021 (YouGov, 2022), a day that then Prime Minister Boris Johnson branded "freedom day". With around 50,000 new cases of Covid-19 each day being reported in the UK at the time, the decision to remove masking mandates (along with a host of other Covid-19 prevention measures) well ahead of most other countries was described as 'dangerous and unethical' by many scientists and medics (BMA, 2021; Gurdasani et al., 2021; Mahase, 2021, p. 1). A rapid return to self-responsibilisation has been identified as part of the neoliberalised response to Covid-19 (Lupton et al., 2021; Kretchmar & Brewer, 2022). And indeed, although mandates were removed in England in July 2021, it remained a government "recommendation" that face masks continue to be worn inside (BBC News, 2021). Mask wearing officially became an individual decision. It also became up to businesses and public services to set their own masking recommendations without the facility to enforce these recommendations (with the exception of a few business and service types). Nevertheless, rates of people who said they had worn a face mask in a public place in the last 7 days remained around 60% after the removal of masking mandates on 19 July 2021 up until the reintroduction of masking mandates between 30 November 2021 and 26 January 2022, during which time masking rates peaked again at 69% (GOV.UK, 2022; YouGov, 2022). This new mandate was introduced in response to the threats posed by the new Omicron variant. However, the lifting of this second mandate in response to the emergence of the "milder" Omicron variant and high vaccine rates signalled a steep decline in masking in the UK, with masking rates falling to 42% by the end of March 2022, and then 21% by June 2022 (YouGov, 2022).

Our book thus covers a period when advice and policy around Covid and masking were in constant flux in the UK and beyond (Qiaoan, 2020). Such uncertainty was a central element of how people experienced the pandemic in general and masking in particular (Zinn & Brown, 2022). Yet, inconsistencies in messaging, ambiguity in how rules were implemented (a characteristic feature of this period in the UK), perceived misalignments between scientific and governmental advice, and the undermining of scientific guidance by politicians, was shown to have sizable consequences on the extent to which people engaged with preventative measures such as masking in the UK and elsewhere (Beaver & Skinner, 2020; Cherry et al., 2021; Zhang et al., 2021; Martin & Vanderslott, 2022).

The centrality of masking to emerging social and scientific discourse meant masking became a way for people to navigate understandings about scientific evidence and knowledge in relation to the Covid-19 pandemic, as well as their trust and affective dispositions regarding political leaders and scientific experts. During the height of the pandemic, people's use of, relationship to, and views on masks were subject to adaptation and negotiation as scientific, legal, political, and moral landscapes surrounding the virus continued to shift. How masking practices were enacted and interpreted were the outcome of these negotiations. We thus understand masking during the pandemic as an everyday material practice through which people made sense of and negotiated different (and changing) knowledges, authorities, and values. In other words, masking became a material conduit through which a great deal of sense-making was channelled. But disagreements and debates around masking, even at times when compliance was high, show us that the changes wrought were partial and contested, and were bounded by uncertainties and political turbulence.

In *Masking in the Pandemic*, we are interested in exploring how, in resolving (or not) uncertainties around masking, people established new ways of doing and being. As we were writing this book, the Covid-19 pandemic shifted into a new phase, which in the UK meant the lifting of all restrictions and a new language of "living with Covid". Then, as we were finalising the manuscript, the WHO declared that Covid-19 was no longer a global health emergency on 5 May 2023. Masking thus offers us an ideal tangible vantage point through which to explore shifting everyday social practice and the remaking of public and moral orders in a period of perhaps unparalleled vicissitudes.

Masking from the Perspective of the Everyday

This book assumes an "everyday life" perspective towards masking, which takes as its point of departure Inglis and Almila's argument that a sociology of masks 'can be particularly attuned to the nuances of everyday practices' (2020, p. 252). The call for a sociological exploration on masking in everyday lives reflects how the broad literature about facemasks during the pandemic focuses predominantly on medical and legal-political dimensions of masking. Face masks are primarily a hygienic intervention, utilised in the pandemic as a medium of protection against spreading Covid-19. But the international nature of masking recommendations, the mandatory way in which masking was stipulated from a governmental level, and the subsequent weaponization of masking by certain political actors and forces, means they also gained political and symbolic significance (Graham et al., 2020). The majority of the literature on masking during the pandemic has consequently focused on medical and political issues (e.g. the preventative efficacy of masks and their appropriate usage, the effectiveness of implemented policies, cross-national comparisons of masking coverage, and the dynamics of scientific and political discourse). Within the human sciences, this has translated (with good reason) into issues of masking being analysed in relation to concepts such as biopolitics and questions of the role and capacities of the modern nation state (Sylvia, 2020; Wu, 2020; Delanty, 2021). Moral issues associated with masking and its implementation have likewise been framed mostly in terms of duties, rights, and bioethics at a supra-individual level (Bos et al., 2020; Khosravi, 2020; Correia et al., 2021; Voinea et al., 2022), or in terms of rationality or psychological moral processing at the level of individual responses to masking (Graham et al., 2020; Chan, 2021; Bruchmann & LaPierre, 2022; Shanka & Gebremariam Kotecho, 2023). All these approaches are of great value to understanding masking. However, such perspectives look past important points about how experiences of masking were lived.

We thus seek to build on sociological work that approaches the topic of masking from the viewpoint of how it shaped social practice in everyday life in the pandemic (e.g. Inglis & Almila, 2020; Lupton et al., 2021). Theoretically, we frame our understanding of the everyday with the help of perspectives in sociology that aim to cultivate sociological attention towards the experiences, relationships, practices, and environments that constitute the contexts of ordinary social life (Back, 2015). For while the everyday is by definition 'at the centre of human existence', its familiarity means its importance is often overlooked, ceded beneath scientific and political discourse in terms of significance, or else subsumed into the purported explanatory power of encompassing social and psychological theories (Pink, 2012, p. 143). Yet everyday life perspectives argue this is mistaken not least because, as the sphere in which the majority of social life is conducted, it is in the interactions in everyday life that practices and experiences are shaped, made sense of, and incorporated into interpretations of how things are. For most people most of the time, the everyday is *the* 'site where experience is made manifest, where it takes shape, where sense is made' (DeNora, 2014, p. xx). Experiences and sense-making are shaped in relation to shared social meaning and social forces, but nonetheless occur at a granular level through a temporal assemblage of circumstances, experiences, and relationships. Understanding the everyday is thus necessary to being 'able to address the question of how [a] sense of reality comes to be generated and how it takes shape, albeit contingently and only for a time' (DeNora, 2014, p. xxi). This point holds a particular resonance for masking. Framed as it was by an assemblage of rapidly changing circumstances and often unclear or incongruous guidance, it was in everyday life where people tried to make sense of how to mask (or not) and what this meant, where knowledges were fumblingly translated into interactions, where interactions produced new modes of practices around masking, where attitudes and impositions were challenged, and where senses of responsibility, discomfort, acquiescence, and resignation were felt.

Sociological focus on the everyday has an established history, with Goffman's gift for 'attentiveness to what is easily discarded as unimportant' prefiguring more recent consolidations of everyday life approaches (Back, 2015, p. 822). Goffman's observational insightfulness into the significance of everyday interactions has been taken by the authors as an inspiration for thinking through how practices of masking developed and were experienced. As well as an acute attentiveness to how interactions unfold, Goffman positioned interactions as integral to the ordering of social experience, with his work bringing to the fore the norms of practice that underpin interactions. As we aim to illuminate throughout this book, key tenets of Goffman's theories were illustrated with a unique intensity by the phenomenon of masking in the pandemic. But the pandemic also brought to the fore a tendency in Goffman's theorising to focus on social norms already in existence. Our focus on masking was partly inspired by our sociological fascination with social change in the making, which was made apparent by the material visibility of masking and the palpable interactional discomfort that this novel practice engendered.

Face masks developed a prominent role in the pandemic as a means to protect oneself and others from the virus, and consequently, as a visible mediator of interactions that allowed interactions and participants in those interactions to be appraised. Goffman (1983) argued that there is generally an "interaction order" to social encounters, and interaction orders are sustained and adjusted as they are participated in by people who attempt to display and appraise awareness of appropriate conduct. Although interaction orders are continually in the making, they tend to have an established inheritance that has generally developed over a significant period of time (Bottero, 2019). While masks were legally stipulated for periods of the pandemic, what proper interactional conduct around masking entailed had little precedent in the UK and other Western contexts. Yet interactional expectations and modes of appraisal quickly developed (aided by the visibility of the mask) in ways that illuminate the significance of everyday interactions to the establishment of wider orders of social practice (discussed in Chaps. 3 and 4 of this book).

Back (2015, p. 820) contends that 'the value of thinking about the everyday is that it […] makes sociologists think about society not as a set of structural arrangements but as a moving and dynamic entity'. We argue that the fluctuating landscape around masking brought into sharp focus what shifting social practice looks like as it was happening in the many aspects of everyday life that it involves. Throughout the book, we develop a relational perspective to explore the relationship between the materiality and moral significance of masking, and how this translated into the development of masking practices in public spaces. From this perspective, we aim to illuminate the interactional development of social norms and practices around masking, and their intersubjective enactment (Emirbayer, 1997; Barnes, 2000; Crossley, 2011; May, 2013). We argue (mostly in Chap. 3) that masking provides a particularly telling example of the significance of disruptions to understanding how social orders are established (Horgan, 2020; Tavory & Fine, 2020). We thus understand masks through the lens of the everyday, which offers potential for profound insight into the nature of changing social practice.

A "Facet" Approach to Exploring Masking

The authors are all members of the Morgan Centre for Research into Everyday Lives. Our writing project began purely with the aim of getting together regularly online to discuss the pandemic and the ongoing changes it wrought in everyday life. Inspired by David Morgan's approach to the many substantive topics he wrote about, including acquaintances, family practices, and snobbery (Morgan, 2009, 2011, 2018), we began to observe and discuss features of the pandemic through the lens of the everyday. Early on, masking became a topic that fascinated us as a tangible, everyday emblem of the pandemic around which new modes of interaction and moral practice were forming. Masking spoke to the authors' shared interests in materiality, relations in public, and morality, and so we decided to start recording our thoughts and observations about experiences of masking as observational texts (Katila et al., 2020), with the general themes of materiality, relations in public, and morality selected as foci for our observations. These were written from the summer of 2020 onwards, initially with the sole intention of forming the basis of the discussions in our meetings. Each of the authors of this book contributed observations about each of these themes.

As the months went on, we began to consider writing about masking in a more systematic manner, which quickly expanded into plans for a book-length text. Our observations inform the basis of the book, with excerpts from these observations (alongside insight from existing empirical studies) used to illustrate our analysis and draw our attention to particular dimensions of masking experiences. Our choice to include such observations is inspired partly by Goffman's (and also David Morgan's) observational sociology and partly by the fact that such approaches have been popular among social scientists trying to make sense of how the nature of social interactions changed during the pandemic, for the most part in relation to social distancing rules (e.g. Collins, 2020; Drury and Stokoe, 2022; Katila et al., 2020; Mehta, 2020). We explored the effects of masking in the broader context of social distancing measures that most governments put in place, and our mode of observation reflects this context. Observational methods are a subset of ethnographic methods (along with participation), but observation is also a more informal way in which sociologists, Goffman and Morgan included, have sought to bring to the fore the often only partially recognised features and textures through which everyday life is lived. We use observations in this latter form, in that our observations were not formally set up, but rather were undertaken as a means to cultivate a 'Goffmanesque attentiveness' (Back, 2015, p. 834) to the experiences and practices of masking that (for a short while) were becoming ordinary features of everyday life in the pandemic. Our observations are drawn from and register our own experiences of masking, while seeking to illustrate features of masking practices in public.

Alongside these observations, our collective writing of this book is underpinned by a "facet methodology" approach, utilised here as a method for thinking that guides our collaboration around the topic of masking. Developed specifically for researching the entangled complexity of everyday life, the aim of facet methodology is to allow social scientists to preserve within their explanations the multidimensional and contingently interconnected nature of relational living (Mason, 2011). It is a research orientation based on a connective ontology, meaning that it does not seek to slice the lived world into different domains, but instead seeks to gain insight into how different aspects of the social world 'are connected and entwined' (Mason, 2011, p. 79). These connections and entwinements can be sought out by selecting investigations, or facets, that focus on strategically 'selected sets of *related* questions, puzzles and problematics' (Mason, 2011, p. 79, emphasis added). When brought together, these facets illuminate something that is more than the sum of its parts. A facet approach thus provides a way of thinking, analysing, and writing that is attuned to '[c]onstellation and association between facets':

> this involves researchers *thinking, imagining and writing their way* across and through different facets and clusters of facets as they follow particular lines of enquiry, and chasing the flashes of insight where they seem to appear (Mason, 2011, p. 81, emphasis added)

The aim of a facet approach is not to seek 'maximum coverage' or to attempt to capture a social phenomenon as fully as possible (Mason, 2011, p. 80). Instead, this research orientation seeks to artfully combine different ways of looking at a topic in an effort to gain insight into the entwined nature of the social world in relation to a particular phenomenon. In this spirit, our book is not meant to constitute an exhaustive empirical study of mask wearing but instead, we use the phenomenon of masking, and strategically selected facets of it, to shed light on the nature of shifting social practice and the interconnectedness of different domains in everyday life. The three facets we chose to focus on (materiality, relations in public, and morality) were combined within a framework of a shared understanding of the significance of the everyday, and an interest in relationality in a broad sense that includes people's relationships with technology and nonhumans. The organising principle in our thinking is an attentiveness to how the selected facets of masking are entangled with each other and how this entwinement informed fluctuating social practices around masking during the pandemic. The different conceptual toolboxes we draw from are thus used to explore the social phenomenon of masking and the changes it has brought about from different angles, allowing us strategic insight into not only masking, but also into how different domains that constitute masking experiences are interconnected.

These different facets of masking practice were considered in relation to each other through both the observations and the writing processes, with each of the authors contributing observations on each of the facets and each author contributing to the writing of each of the chapters. This has allowed us to draw out the entwined nature of masking through a process of collaborative writing that emerged through collaborative observation. We are mindful that our positionality has shaped the writing of this book, most obviously in our observations that formed the basis for this writing project. We are all white academics based in the UK, who were observing the domestic and immediate neighbouring spaces we were in. Over time, as our project grew into a book, we consciously and systematically engaged with other sources that documented the racialised, classed, gendered, and able-centric nature of the pandemic. This has allowed us to keep in view how existing inequalities were refracted through debates over and practices in masking.

The Layout of the Book

The chapters that follow focus on the three facets—materiality, relations in public, and morality—in turn, while illuminating connections between them. The concluding chapter discusses what the three facets, when brought together, illuminate about masking, social practice, and also uncertainty during the pandemic.

Chapter 2 Masks and Materiality

Chapter 2 unpacks the materiality of masks, drawing on theoretical positions which highlight the hybridity of things/people (Latour, 1993) and the material effects and possibilities of masks. New materialist approaches (such as Boscagli, 2014; Coole & Frost, 2010; Smelik, 2018) are instructive in thinking about masking in ways that open up the complex materialities of masks and the relations between materiality, human actors, and nonhuman features of the lived world (such as viruses). New materialism centres on "matter", covering both material matter and matter in the sense of being important, significant, or having meaning. These approaches allow an understanding of the relations between elements in masking (the synthetic or cotton fibres, breath, the face) and how these become entwined in relations with other elements. We explore how a mask is a thing in relation to other things, as well as being a set of material practices, here referred to as "masking". Visibly worn on our faces, masks became part of how everyday relations between people were (and are) mediated. The visibility and aesthetics of the mask can be seen as ways in which anxieties about the pandemic were engaged with (e.g. avoiding the unmasked, or as a performative gesture showing to others our own position, something that we discuss in more depth in Chap. 4 in relation to morality).

This approach to masks and masking also facilitates an understanding of masking as part of social relations, including how existing divisions and inequalities were exacerbated. We build on these ideas to think through how the materiality of the masks connect to experiences of comfort and discomfort, both physical and social (Miller & Woodward, 2012). We draw from Sara Ahmed's (2014) observation that we tend not to notice what is comfortable, unless this is disrupted and we come to feel discomfort where bodies feel out of place, emerging as an 'acute awareness of the surface of one's body […] when one cannot inhabit the social skin, which is shaped by some bodies, and not others' (Ahmed, 2014, p. 148). The materiality of masks makes manifest feelings of marginality or discomfort (Jenss & Hofmann, 2021). Whilst the sudden shift to masking practices in 2020 was a shift for many to feeling uncomfortable in public places, Ahmed's writing illuminates that many people already felt ill at ease and were already subjected to the negative gaze and discomfort of being in certain public spaces. Encountering this for the first time when wearing a face mask thus highlights racialised and other privileges in how social space is experienced. To think this through, we draw on parallel literature on veiling; the Islamic veil is 'semiotically overcharged' (Tarlo, 2007, p. 135), politicised, and hyper-visible (Lewis, 2015). We use Tarlo's idea of the 'resonances' of veils (Tarlo, 2007) to think about the resonances of masking as how people experience and live the multiple meanings the mask has.

Chapter 3 Masking and the (Re)making of the Public Realm

In this chapter, we develop further the notion of masks as material things that mediate relations between people. Given that masking was for a while mandatory in many public settings in the UK, our focus lies on relations in public. Extending Goffman's work on how public order is regulated in face-to-face interaction and the patterned behaviour that results (Goffman, 1963, 1967, 1971), we are interested in exploring *how* social order and rules of interaction became established in a situation where people had to figure out anew how to interact with others in public (Inglis & Almila, 2020; Sikka, 2021). But beyond an interest in how people dealt with the interactional uncertainties that masking gave rise to, we are also fascinated with how people responded to the masking practices of those around them and how this shaped interactional dis/comfort during the pandemic. We argue that this provides telling insights into the generative role that disruption plays in the (re-)establishing of the interaction order (see Horgan, 2020; Tavory & Fine, 2020).

The chapter also illuminates how masks operated as objects that brought to light the existing and newly forming boundaries of social cohesion and hierarchy that underpin social space (Pfaller, 2020). The notion of a "stranger" gained new negative undertones as a potential source of infection, and wearing or not wearing a mask could lead to a person becoming the target of intense scrutiny, impoliteness, and even aggression (Iranmanesh & Alpar Atun, 2021; Van Gorp, 2021). Our interest lies in understanding the existing and newly emerging social hierarchies that masking made visible particularly around race, gender, age and dis/ability. In addition, we consider the Eurocentric notions of "face" that informed much of the public and academic discussions in Western contexts about the impact of masking on face-to-face interaction.

We propose that paying attention to interactional uncertainty, discomfort, and the power dynamics that underpin how these are negotiated offers a way of understanding how new interaction orders are established. We build on these thoughts in Chap. 4, which explores how new moral norms around masking were negotiated in everyday life.

Chapter 4 Masks, Lay Moralities, and Moral Practice

The relationship masking has with protecting health means it developed as a moral issue and, for many people, as a fundamentally moral practice around which "lay moralities" were constructed. We argue here that masking illuminates important points about how lay moralities and moral practices are constructed and enacted in ways that were of deep significance to people during the pandemic, but which are mostly overlooked in dominant social scientific interpretations of masking. Social scientific interpretations of masking have tended to reduce people's ordinary normative evaluations to being the consequence of institutional imposition on the one hand, or pre-orientated moral dispositions or psychological "moral foundations" on the other (for account of such tendencies in how social scientists discuss moral matters, see Sayer (2011)). These positions look past how interactionally moulded orders of moral practice around masking developed, which engendered emergent modes of enacting, appraising, and contesting "proper" masking conduct. A key argument for this chapter, then, is that masking during the pandemic should be considered as an interactional moral phenomena. Moral practices of masking developed in relation to unfolding knowledges that moulded new norms of conduct and senses of responsibility, which had to be figured out in relation to the visible materiality of the mask as a particularly interactional moral thing.

These points will be discussed in relation to the assumption of moralised positions towards masking, the social proliferation of masking, how moral practices were enacted across different situations, how uncertainties and power imbalances led to opacities in practices in masking in relation to feelings of what the "right thing to do" is, and how negotiations of rules and contestations were a regular feature of masking as a moral practice. Alongside this, and referring back to the previous chapter on relations in public, we explore the moral policing and judgement exhibited in the interaction orders that developed around masking.

While social and scientific discourses led to mask wearing becoming what many people took to be the "proper thing to do", such discourses became something of a fault line, a visible marker for "us" and "them" (see Southerton (2002) for discussion of moral boundary drawing). As several have noted (Chan, 2021; Graham et al., 2020), these divisions in attitudes towards masking often align with Jonathon Haidt's (2013) "moral foundations theory" arguments for explaining political and moral divisions in Western societies. As such, moral foundations theory has become the predominant means through which moral attitudes towards masking have been analysed (e.g. Bruchmann & LaPierre, 2022; Chan, 2021; Graham et al., 2020). While we agree that moral judgement is socially intuitive before it is rational (Haidt, 2013), we argue that moral foundations theory looks past how lay moralities around masking were constructed in relation to mobile social discourse, and how these lay moralities were translated into and further moulded by the development of moral norms of action and modes of judgement.

Chapter 5 Conclusion: Masks and Uncertainty

While the chapters above remain attuned to the overlaps and crossovers between them, in this concluding chapter we look at the three facets in the round. One of the notable themes running throughout the book, which is used to connect the facets by way of conclusion, is uncertainty. Mask wearing practices are a useful lens to understand approaches to uncertainty, as material, moral, and interactional conventions changed in relation to, but not dictated by, public scientific knowledge and governmental rules. This final chapter will consider what these facets, when taken together, tell us about masking, its role in everyday sense making at times of profound uncertainty, and how the various material features of masks facilitated the shifting interactional and moral meanings with which they became imbued. We argue this illuminates the entanglement of everyday meanings and interactions with the material world, social discourse, practices, and vulnerabilities. Likewise, we discuss how practices of masking provide broader sociological insights into changing social practices at times of social turbulence. The conclusion also considers the changing fate of masking in the UK as a practice that has declined, but which still constitutes a feature of social life that is still intermittently visible.

References

Ahmed, S. (2014). *The cultural politics of emotion*. Edinburgh University Press.

Back, L. (2015). Why everyday life matters: Class, community and making life Livable. *Sociology, 49*(5), 820–836.

Barnes, B. (2000). *Understanding agency: Social theory and responsible action*. SAGE.

BBC News. (2020). Coronavirus: Do face masks work? *BBC News*. Retrieved April 26, 2023, from https://www.bbc.co.uk/news/av/health-51881555

BBC News. (2021, July 11). Covid-19: Masks still expected to be worn indoors after 19 July—Zahawi. *BBC News*. Retrieved April 26, 2023, from https://www.bbc.com/news/uk-57795409

Beaver, K., & Skinner, G. (2020). *Government advice could change Britons' attitudes to wearing facemasks, Ipsos MORI*. Retrieved July 1, 2021, from https://www.ipsos.com/ipsos-mori/en-uk/government-advice-could-change-britons-attitudes-wearing-facemasks

Blackburn, P. (2020). *Government makes wearing face masks mandatory, The British Medical Association*. Retrieved April 26, 2023, from https://www.bma.org.uk/news-and-opinion/government-makes-wearing-face-masks-mandatory

BMA. (2021). *Pressing ahead with lifting final restrictions in England on July 19 is 'irresponsible and perilous', says BMA—BMA media centre—BMA, The British Medical Association is the trade union and professional body for doctors in the UK*. Retrieved April 26, 2023, from https://www.bma.org.uk/bma-media-centre/pressing-ahead-with-lifting-final-restrictions-in-england-on-july-19-is-irresponsible-and-perilous-says-bma

Bos, B., Drupp, M. A., Meya, J. N., & Quaas, M. F. (2020). Moral suasion and the private provision of public goods: Evidence from the COVID-19 pandemic. *Environmental and Resource Economics, 76*(4), 1117–1138.

Boscagli, M. (2014). *Stuff theory: Everyday objects and radical materialism.* Bloomsbury.

Bottero, W. (2019). *A sense of inequality.* Rowman & Littlefield.

Bruchmann, K., & LaPierre, L. (2022). Moral foundations predict perceptions of moral permissibility of COVID-19 public health guideline violations in United States university students. *Frontiers in Psychology, 12.*

Chan, E. Y. (2021). Moral foundations underlying behavioral compliance during the COVID-19 pandemic. *Personality and Individual Differences, 171,* 110463.

Chang, H. J., Min, S., Woo, H., & Yurchisin, J. (2021). Mask-wearing behavior during the COVID-19 pandemic: A cross-cultural comparison between the United States and South Korea. *Family and Consumer Sciences Research Journal, 50*(1), 5–26.

Cherry, T. L., James, A. G., & Murphy, J. (2021). The impact of public health messaging and personal experience on the acceptance of mask wearing during the COVID-19 pandemic. *Journal of Economic Behavior & Organization, 187,* 415–430.

Collins, R. (2020). Social distancing as a critical test of the micro-sociology of solidarity. *American Journal of Cultural Sociology, 8*(3), 477–497.

Coole, D., & Frost, S. (Eds.). (2010). *New materialisms: Ontology, agency, and politics.* Duke University Press.

Correia, M., Rego, G., & Nunes, R. (2021). The right to be forgotten and COVID-19: Privacy versus public interest. *Acta Bioethica, 27*(1), 59–67.

Crossley, N. (2011). *Towards relational sociology.* Routledge.

Delanty, G. (2021). *Pandemics, politics, and society: Critical perspectives on the Covid-19 crisis.* De Gruyter.

DeNora, T. (2014). *Making sense of reality: Culture and perception in everyday life.* SAGE.

Dillard, J. P., Tian, X., Cruz, S. M., Smith, R. A., & Shen, L. (2021). Persuasive messages, social norms, and reactance: A study of masking behavior during a COVID-19 campus health campaign. *Health Communication, 0*(0), 1–11. https://doi.org/10.1080/10410236.2021.2007579

Drury, J., & Stokoe, E. (2022). The interactional production and breach of new norms in the time of COVID-19: Achieving physical distancing in public spaces. *British Journal of Social Psychology, 61*(3), 971–990.

Emirbayer, M. (1997). Manifesto for a relational sociology. *American Journal of Sociology, 103*(2), 281–317.

Goffman, E. (1963). *Behavior in public places: Notes on the social Organization of Gatherings.* Free Press.

Goffman, E. (1967). *Interaction ritual: Essays on face-to-face behavior.* Pantheon Books.

Goffman, E. (1971). *Relations in public: Microstudies of the public order.* Basic Books.

Goffman, E. (1983). The interaction order: American Sociological Association, 1982 presidential address. *American Sociological Review, 48*(1), 1–17.

GOV.UK. (2020, April 21). *DELVE: Report on face masks for the general public.* GOV.UK. Retrieved April 26, 2023, from https://www.gov.uk/government/publications/delve-report-on-face-masks-for-the-general-public-21-april-2020

GOV.UK. (2022). *England returns to Plan A as regulations on face coverings and COVID Passes change today.* GOV.UK. Retrieved April 26, 2023, from https://www.gov.uk/government/news/england-returns-to-plan-a-as-regulations-on-face-coverings-and-covid-passes-change-today

Goyes, D. R., South, N., Ramos Ñeñetofe, D. T., Cuchimba, A., Baicué, P., & Abaibira, M. A. (2022). 'An incorporeal disease': COVID-19, social trauma and health injustice in four Colombian indigenous communities. *The Sociological Review 71*(1). https://doi.org/10.1177/00380261221133673

Graham, A., Cullen, F. T., Pickett, J. T., Jonson, C. L., Haner, M., & Sloan, M. M. (2020). Faith in trump, moral foundations, and social distancing Defiance during the coronavirus pandemic. *Socius, 6.*

Greenhalgh, T. (2020). Laying straw men to rest: author's reply to "urgency and uncertainty: Covid-19, face masks, and evidence informed policy". *BMJ, 369*, m2240. https://doi.org/10.1136/bmj.m2240

Gurdasani, D., Drury, J., Greenhalgh, T., Griffin, S., Haque, Z., Hyde, Z., Katzourakis, A., McKee, M., Michie, S., Pagel, C., & Reicher, S. (2021). Mass infection is not an option: We must do more to protect our young. *The Lancet, 398*(10297), 297–298.

Haidt, J. (2013). *The righteous mind: Why good people are divided by politics and religion.* Penguin.

Horgan, M. (2020). Urban interaction ritual: Strangership, civil inattention and everyday incivilities in public space. *Pragmatics, 30*(1), 116–141. John Benjamins.

Inglis, D., & Almila, A.-M. (2020). Un-masking the mask: Developing the sociology of facial politics in pandemic times and after. *SocietàMutamentoPolitica, 11*(21), 251–257.

Iranmanesh, A., & Alpar Atun, R. (2021). Reading the changing dynamic of urban social distances during the COVID-19 pandemic via twitter. *European Societies, 23*(supl), S872–S886.

Jenss, H., & Hofmann, V. (Eds.). (2021). *Fashion and materiality: Cultural practices in global contexts.* Bloomsbury Publishing.

Katila, J., Gan, Y., & Goodwin, M. H. (2020). Interaction rituals and 'social distancing': New haptic trajectories and touching from a distance in the time of COVID-19. *Discourse Studies, 22*(4), 418–440.

Khosravi, H. (2020). Protecting the human rights of individuals against Covid-19 (coronavirus) in the light of Kant's deontological moral philosophy. *Journal of Philosophical Investigations, 14*(31), 195–219.

Kretchmar, K., & Brewer, T. J. (2022). Neoliberalism, COVID, anti-science, and the politics of school reopening. *Education Policy Analysis Archives, 30*(42).

Lam, S. K. K., Hung, M. S. Y., & Chien, W. T. (2020). Uncertainty surrounding the use of face masks in the community amid the COVID-19 pandemic. *International Journal of Nursing Studies, 108*(103651). https://doi.org/10.1016/j.ijnurstu.2020.103651

Latour, B. (1993). *We have never been modern*. Harvard University Press.

Lewis, R. (2015). Uncovering modesty: Dejabis and dewigies expanding the parameters of the modest fashion blogosphere. *Fashion Theory, 19*(2), 243–269.

Lupton, D., Southerton, C., Clark, M., & Watson, A. (2021). *The face mask in COVID times: A Sociomaterial analysis, the face mask in COVID times*. De Gruyter.

Mahase, E. (2021). Covid-19: Experts condemn UK "freedom day" as dangerous and unethical. *BMJ, 374*, n1829.

Martin, G. P., Hanna, E., & Dingwall, R. (2020). Urgency and uncertainty: Covid-19, face masks, and evidence informed policy. *BMJ: British Medical Journal (Online), 369*.

Martin, S., & Vanderslott, S. (2022). "Any idea how fast 'It's just a mask!' Can turn into 'It's just a vaccine!'": From mask mandates to vaccine mandates during the COVID-19 pandemic. *Vaccine, 40*(51), 7488–7499.

Mason, J. (2011). Facet methodology: The case for an inventive research orientation. *Methodological Innovations Online, 6*(3), 75–92.

May, V. (2013). *Connecting self to society: Belonging in a changing world*. Palgrave.

Mehta, V. (2020). The new proxemics: COVID-19, social distancing, and sociable space. *Journal of Urban Design, 25*(6), 669–674.

Miller, D., & Woodward, S. (2012). *Blue jeans: The art of the ordinary*. University of California Press.

Morgan, D. H. J. (2009). *Acquaintances: The space between intimates and strangers*. Open University Press.

Morgan, D. H. J. (2011). *Rethinking family practices*. Palgrave Macmillan.

Morgan, D. H. J. (2018). *Snobbery*. Policy Press.

Pfaller, L. (2020). Theorizing the virus: Abjection and the COVID-19 pandemic. *International Journal of Sociology and Social Policy, 40*(9/10), 821–829.

Pink, S. (2012). *Situating everyday life: Practices and places*. SAGE.

Qian, Y., & Fuller, S. (2020). COVID-19 and the gender employment gap among parents of Young children. *Canadian Public Policy, 46*(S2), S89–S101.

Qiaoan, R. (2020). The myth of masks: A tale of risk selection in the COVID-19 pandemic. *Social Anthropology, 28*(2), 336–337.

Reuters. (2020, April 3). No evidence that masks worn by healthy people affect coronavirus spread—UK official. *Reuters*. Retrieved April 26, 2023, from https://www.reuters.com/article/uk-health-coronavirus-britain-masks-idUKKBN21L2OW

Sayer, A. (2011). *Why things matter to people: Social science, values and ethical life.* Cambridge University Press.

Shanka, M. S., & Gebremariam Kotecho, M. (2023). Combining rationality with morality—Integrating theory of planned behavior with norm activation theory to explain compliance with COVID-19 prevention guidelines. *Psychology, Health & Medicine, 28*(2), 305–315.

Sikka, T. (2021). Feminist materialism and Covid-19: The agential activation of everyday objects. *NORA—Nordic Journal of Feminist and Gender Research, 29*(1), 4–16.

Smelik, A. (2018). New materialism: A theoretical framework for fashion in the age of technological innovation. *International Journal of Fashion Studies, 5*(1), 33–54.

Smith, M. (2020). *COVID-19: Britons still won't wear face masks. YouGov.* https://yougov.co.uk/topics/health/articles-reports/2020/06/04/covid-19-britons-still-wont-wear-face-masks

Southerton, D. (2002). Boundaries of 'us' and 'them': Class, mobility and identification in a new town. *Sociology, 36*(1), 171–193.

Sylvia, J. J. (2020). The biopolitics of social distancing. *Social Media + Society, 6*(3), 2056305120947661.

Tarlo, E. (2007). Hijab in London: Metamorphosis, resonance and effects. *Journal of Material Culture, 12*(2), 131–156.

Tateo, L. (2021). Face masks as layers of meaning in times of COVID-19. *Culture & Psychology, 27*(1), 131–151.

Tavory, I., & Fine, G. A. (2020). Disruption and the theory of the interaction order. *Theory and Society, 49*(3), 365–385.

The Independent. (2020, March 12). Face masks could increase risk of getting coronavirus, medical chief warns. *The Independent.* Retrieved April 26, 2023, from https://www.independent.co.uk/news/health/coronavirus-news-face-masks-increase-risk-infection-doctor-jenny-harries-a9396811.html

The Royal Society. (2020). *Face masks and coverings for the general public: Behavioural knowledge, effectiveness of cloth coverings and public messaging.* The Royal Society.

Van Gorp, B. (2021). Face masks as floating signifiers during the COVID-19 pandemic in Belgium. *Visual Studies, 36*(2), 124–132.

Voinea, C., Wangmo, T., & Vică, C. (2022). Respecting older adults: Lessons from the COVID-19 pandemic. *Journal of Bioethical Inquiry, 19*(2), 213–223.

World Health Organization. (2020a, June 5). *Advice on the use of masks in the context of COVID-19: interim guidance.* WHO/2019-nCoV/IPC_Masks/2020.4. World Health Organization. Retrieved April 26, 2023, from https://apps.who.int/iris/handle/10665/332293

World Health Organization (2020b, April 6). *Advice on the use of masks in the context of COVID-19, Interim guidance.* Retrieved April 26, 2023, from

https://apps.who.int/iris/bitstream/handle/10665/331693/WHO-2019-nCov-IPC_Masks-2020.3-eng.pdf?sequence=1&isAllowed=y
Wu, Y. (2020). Witnessing the pandemic with Foucault: Power, politics, and COVID-19. *Canadian Social Science, 16*(8), 36–40.
YouGov. (2022). *Personal measures taken to avoid COVID-19 | YouGov*. Retrieved March 15, 2023, from https://yougov.co.uk/topics/international/articles-reports/2020/03/17/personal-measures-taken-avoid-covid-19
Zhang, Y. S. D., Young Leslie, H., Sharafaddin-Zadeh, Y., Noels, K., & Lou, N. M. (2021). Public health messages about face masks early in the COVID-19 pandemic: Perceptions of and impacts on Canadians. *Journal of Community Health, 46*(5), 903–912.
Zinn, J. O., & Brown, P. R. (2022). COVID-19 risks: Dynamics of culture and inequality across six continents. In P. R. Brown & J. O. Zinn (Eds.), *Covid-19 and the sociology of risk and uncertainty: Studies of social phenomena and social theory across 6 continents* (pp. 1–26). Springer.

CHAPTER 2

Masks and Materiality

Abstract This chapter explores the multiple materialities of masks, drawing from Mol, to think about how masks come into being through the practices in which they are implicated and how those practices are related to one another. We draw from new materialist perspectives to think about the relations between material elements, as well as between humans and nonhumans. A mask is a thing made up of multiple elements (fabric, breath, viruses); it exists in relation to other things, and comprises a set of material practices (here referred to as "masking"), which open up relations between people. In this chapter, we consider how masks are interesting materially, and how using materiality as a lens to think about masking facilitates insights into the relationships that masks allow (social, material, and personal), and the significance of material things to interactional practice. The chapter explores masking in terms of different types of masks, the fashion and aesthetics of masking, and how this affects their "afterlives". We finish the chapter with a discussion of comfort and discomfort as material and social, and explore this through analogies with practices of veiling to think about who is made visible by masking and with what consequences.

Keywords Masks • Materiality • New Materialism • Sense making • Aesthetics • Relationality • Comfort and discomfort

O. Abbott et al., *Masking in the Pandemic*, Consumption and Public Life, https://doi.org/10.1007/978-3-031-45781-4_2

What Are Masks? Thinking Through Materiality

What is a face mask? In the context of the Covid-19 pandemic, the answer may seem self-evident: it is a fabric covering that goes over the mouth and nose and is fitted by loops behind the ears or around the back of the head. The purpose of the mask is to filter exhaled and inhaled air to limit the diffusion of, in the case of Covid-19, a virus. In other contexts, face masks could be worn to limit the amount of particulate pollution breathed in, or to protect from fine dust or other particulates during construction. Many forms of masks have respiratory filters and eye covers. In the present discussion, we focus on forms of face masks which proliferated during the Covid-19 pandemic.

When we think more about the forms that masks took in the pandemic, there was significant variance in what the mask was made of (such as cotton fabric, synthetic plastic fibres such as polypropylene), its appearance, but also how it was worn. Consider one of the ways that people could wear masks: the often-observed practice of tucking the mask under the chin so it was still on the head, but no longer covering the nose or mouth. It is still a face mask, but it would not provide any sort of barrier to microscopic particles and therefore not disrupt transmission of the virus. It no longer has the intended function of the pandemic mask, even if we recognise it as a mask. This means we can understand masks as "multiple" in practice. We draw this point from Mol (2002), who shows that an object that might be considered singular in theory turns out to be multiple in practice. This ontology is used throughout this chapter for thinking about masks because it allows masks to be simultaneously different things in different practices—in health and medicine, fashion, public interaction, politics, and so on. Masks therefore come into being through the practices in which they are implicated and how those practices are related to one another.

If we now revisit the opening lay definition of a mask, where its purpose is to filter inhaled and exhaled air, masks exist in relation to the air that surrounds and passes through them, the bodies wearing them, the people seeing them. Even when they are not worn, whether stuffed in a pocket or in a drawer of rarely used things, masks always exist in relation to other things. In this chapter, we develop these ways of thinking about the materiality of masks to open up the relations of masks and masking. A mask is a thing, it is in relation to other things, as well as being a set of material practices, here referred to as "masking". In this chapter, we begin to unpick these different dimensions of masking. In the introduction, we made a case for why masks are interesting sociologically. Here we consider how masks are interesting materially, and how using materiality as a lens to think about masking facilitates insights into the relationships that masks allow (social, material, and personal), and the significance of material things to interactional practice.

This chapter starts with a discussion of how meanings and masking co-emerged in the pandemic. We discuss how masks were used to make sense of the pandemic and the changing social world it engendered in relation to the unfamiliarities of masking for many. The chapter then moves to an exploration of what masking can be. In taking an approach that centres masking practices, we simultaneously decentre the object (Law, 2002) of masks by considering masking as materially multiple. We then move on to explore this through the different materials of masks, relations between homemade and medical grade masks, and the effects this has on the "after-lives" of masks. We explore the multiple relationalities of masks which sets up the relational approach of the book, including the mask as a set of relations in itself (materials, breath, viruses), the mask in relation to other things, as well as how the mask instantiates relations between people. We finish the chapter with a discussion of comfort and discomfort as material and social, and explore this through analogies with practices of veiling. This allows us to scrutinise continuities in inequalities of who is made visible and with what consequences, and also the connections between being made visible and how people cultivate their sense of self and who they are.

Making Sense of Masks and Making Sense with Masks

As academics we try to make sense of the world through our research and writing; in this book, we are thinking *about* and *with* face masks. But we argue here that people also thought with masks in their everyday lives as a way to make sense of the pandemic and the changing world they found themselves in (see Miller & Woodward, 2007 on how material culture is involved in "making sense of"). Thinking about which masks to buy, and how, when, and where to wear them were all important ways in which people materially engaged with Covid-19 and the changing social, political, and legal implications of the pandemic. The pandemic was marked by unusual degrees of uncertainty with competing advice, knowledges, and anxieties. Whilst there was volubility of public debate on the pandemic and masks, which was evident in people's everyday discussions, people were also making sense of and negotiating these changes and anxieties as they put on, wore, or did not wear masks. Indeed, masks emerged as a medium through which people negotiated normative ideas about pandemic restrictions, including who should be wearing masks (discussed further in Chap. 4). Part of this making sense involved (particularly in contexts where masking was a novel practice) becoming familiar with the experience of masking. In many countries—such as some East Asian countries—masking practices were already prevalent, although these practices changed and shifted in the pandemic. However, in countries such as the UK where masks were far less familiar, masking took a significant amount of getting used to, with the materiality of masking meaning its strangeness was a physical experience:

> *Vanessa (January 2021): The first time I wore a mask, I felt like I was suffocating, and even though I wasn't wearing glasses, I could have sworn that my eyes were misting up. Since then, I've got a bit more used to wearing a mask, though my nose still runs like a tap and as I step outside the shop or train station and pull my mask off, I relish the cool breeze on my damp chin, nose and cheeks.*

Such experiences of masking were often beset with contradictions. As Sophie noted in her observations, although masking in public provided a sense of safety, the affective and material aspects of a mundane activity like visiting a shop were disrupted by its relation to masking:

> *Sophie (January, 2021): only being worn occasionally (such as on a trip to the shops) means that [masks] are then experienced as alien to the wearer as they have a self-conscious relationship to the mask. Masks may be both familiar and strange through the material relationships wearers have to masks; you wear a mask for an hour in a supermarket and then in taking it off feel its absence.*

Consequently, one way we think about materiality is in terms of the (un)familiarity of masking. Indeed, thinking about the materiality of masks, as closely fitting to the face (to be effective), it is evident that we need to consider the practices of wearing masks as embodied. However, familiarity and unfamiliarity is not just about the relationship the mask has to the body. It also points towards how we think about how material culture can, in Miller's (1997) reworking of Gombrich, frame and shape our everyday lives and experiences. Often the less we notice objects (e.g. wallets, keys) the more important they may be in framing our everyday lives and experiences. These perspectives are useful in helping to understand ubiquitous forms of material culture (as masks became during the pandemic). Yet, masks were in the unusual position of being ubiquitous and also still new and in many ways unfamiliar. And when we start to think about the daily wearing of masks, the diversity of different types of masks (fabric, medical), and also practices of wearing across different spaces (discussed further in Chap. 3), then it is evident that our relationship to the familiar/unfamiliarity of masks was (and is) shifting and dynamic.

Theorising Multiple Materialities of Masks

An instructive approach to thinking about masking in a way that opens up the complex materialities of masks and the relations between material elements of masks is new materialism (such as Boscagli, 2014; Coole & Frost, 2010). New materialism centres "matter" (entailing a shift away from discrete objects) including minerals, synthetics, and so on. For Bennett (2010), matter is vibrant, and matter encompasses objects, people and environments. Thinking about masking in this way, masks are not solely an object (the mask) but rather multiple forms of matter, such as the fabric we breathe through, the ties around our ears, our breath, the virus. Positions such as Bennett's allow us to think about agency in more distributed ways based upon an understanding of the relations between elements in masking (the synthetic or cotton fibres, breath, the face). It has long been a position of material culture studies that agency cannot be reduced to the actions and intentions of an individual human (as developed, for example, in Gell, 1998). Objects are not passive in carrying meanings, but instead through their materiality are agentic (Gell, 1998) and the meanings and societal implications of objects is neither determined by things and their properties nor is it imposed by people. Instead, meanings, moralities, selfhood, and social relations are co-constituted by people and things (Miller, 2005). Masks are designed to limit the spread of Covid-19. Yet there are unintended effects such as the misting of glasses and the wearer feeling hot or damp-faced. Positions such as Bennett's allow us to think through how agency emerges from the assemblages of matter. In the case of masks this includes 'the textility of the garment to the tactility of the human body' (Smelik, 2018, p. 34). Thinking about the agency of masking means that whilst we here centre the mask in this book, we can also decentre it by thinking about multiple materialities.

Interweaving strands of social and political theory have wrestled with nonhuman agency and attempted to find ways to redistribute agency.

Michael Serres' (1982) work shows how objects only get their meanings in practical contexts. Using the example of a ball game, he argues that the game is focused on the material ball which gives a player particular capacities—to score or pass—but also marks them as the target to be tackled. Masks too create new capacities in contexts and comparably mark people (or not) for different kinds of actions. In this regard, the agency of masks emerges as a 'dance' (Pickering, 1995) where there's a back and forth in terms of who or what is leading the show, which depends on the agendas and capacities of the actors.

Agency distributed through human and nonhuman matter and forces can be understood as *liveliness*, an insight emerging from Haraway's (1985) feminist philosophy of science, that has found recent resurgence and consideration within new materialist positions (Coole & Frost, 2010). Matter is alive and 'becomes' with us (St. Pierre et al., 2016, p. 101), it is not something we act upon but instead is lively. And so, when we consider everyday actions through something such as facemasks, we are not just looking at the decisions and actions of people, but also at the effects masks have, which become part of embodied decision-making processes. Such processes are mostly not considered in the abstract. Instead, when wearing a mask, we may start to feel hot and anxious. We react to the visibility of the mask on someone's face as part of how we behave in relation to them. As discussed further in Chap. 3, with masking, expressive capacities change, including greater emphasis on the eyes and people doing expressions behind masks and other more pronounced bodily gestures to convey emotion. For example, smiling broadly raises the cheeks. When wearing a mask, the mask lifts and pulls tighter across a face, and a new expression is created. Likewise, there was the potential for masks to hide expressiveness, allowing people to privately express feelings they hoped were not interpreted. These capacities emerged through the practices of masking, as people interacted and learnt to perform emotions and interpret and read "expressive masks" (Crandall et al., 2022). Masks thus generate affects and change what the human-mask assemblage can accomplish.

This also means that people and masks relate in particular ways. Masks can draw particular attention to the parts of the face. Taking fit and sizing as an example, smaller masks felt restrictive, inhibiting breathing and talking, painful even behind the ears or creating pressure under the eyes. In contrast, too large a mask was difficult to keep in place, slipping over the nose, and people had to open their jaw to try to "hold" it on their face (Sharma et al., 2020). In both cases, and with masking more generally, people took to adjusting their masks—regularly touching their facial area—thereby bringing various particles closer to their mouths and noses. In other words, redistributing the mode of infection from airborne particles to touching through physical means (avoiding touching the face mask once worn was a key part of masking advice that many found hard to follow) (Sharma et al., 2020). Thus, the materialities of masks in practice, while mandated in order to reduce viral transmission, could enact a contrary process that raised the possibilities for the virus to gather on mask fabrics.

The mask exists and is enacted here through how people related to them on their faces. This relation also happened through the kinds of masks people chose, how they wore them, and what was possible through wearing them. Karin Knorr Cetina (2001, p. 185) uses the term 'objectual relations' to capture the process of relating to epistemic objects—open-ended, ever-changing objects. This is very much a shift in descriptive approach from a performative idiom to a relational one. The ideas emerge from a 'postsocial' approach, which aims to expand the analytical frame of relations from a sociality focused on humans. Masks can be fruitfully understood through this form of epistemic relation, where masks can be considered open-ended and signifying; they change materially and conceptually, and the changes point us towards different actions (e.g. choosing the right-sized masks, or one made from appropriate materials, or choosing between a mask that was more comfortable versus one that was seen as more protective depending on the circumstances in which they were to be worn). Our knowledge of how they worked in relation to expression, breathing, glasses, preventing viral transmission, and so on, was continually changing. People found themselves in different contexts and settings where the capacities had to be worked out *with* and *through* the materiality of masks, bodies, hot breath, cold air, and so on. The ways masks sat on faces, changed experiences, and the changing knowledge about Covid-19 and the efficacy of masking, meant that relations to masks were ever-shifting. Indeed, continual change was a core aspect of masking. As discussed in the next chapter, theories of practice are often critiqued for an overemphasis on stability, resulting in accounts of the role of change to practices being less well developed. Examining masking, and the emerging relations to masks, therefore becomes a material way into understanding how practices arise, take shape, and in this case ebb, and the material-discursive resources in these processes. In the next section, we begin to explore the "downtimes" of masking.

Homemade or Medical? The Aesthetics of Masks and Their Former Lives and Afterlives

So far, we have discussed the materiality of masks mostly in terms of being worn on the body, and yet masks spend a great deal of time unworn (in pockets, in bags, being washed) as well as having histories and afterlives. Towards the start of the pandemic, in the UK and elsewhere, there was a significant shortage of medical grade masks, even for those working in health settings. Consequently, as the efficacy of facemasks became more clear, early periods of the pandemic saw a significant trend of people making their own masks, as well as fashion companies and companies that usually made other products creating and marketing face masks (Lupton et al., 2021). The aesthetics of these homemade or commercially made fabric masks became a key part of masking early on. The making of homemade masks was facilitated by a proliferation of "how to" videos on YouTube (Keough, 2021), and developed into small-scale businesses where people bought inventively designed masks on sites such as Etsy. This occurred amongst contested information about whether cloth masks were worth wearing for protection or not (Sharma et al., 2020). This was a significant area of technical contestation for people to navigate, which became part of how people interacted with each other. At the start of the pandemic as masking was being increasingly recommended but shortages of medical grade masks were reported, the cloth mask was perhaps taken as a sign of someone who was taking the pandemic seriously, but later perhaps became a sign of someone not taking updated guidance on masking seriously enough.

Nevertheless, where a mask came from impacts on its afterlife. As Keough (2021) notes homemade or gifted masks had a different afterlife to a medical grade one, with a homemade or gifted mask more likely to be kept, even if no longer worn, as they became part of the cycles of laundering clothing and fabrics within the home. Sophie, one of the authors of this book, for example, bought her youngest child a superhero-themed cotton mask, which he was so enthusiastic about that it became part of his ninja outfit. Its connection to being a mask to limit the chances of him getting Covid-19 has all but disappeared. Now, the mask has moved into the fancy dress drawer alongside pirate costumes and other superhero outfits.

Likewise, although medical-grade masks are meant to be disposable, they also live on in terms of being binned and not recyclable. Indeed, the very reason that masks needed to be washed or disposed of is directly related to their intended function. By filtering viral (and other particles) from exhaled and inhaled air, they become a site for collecting those very viral particles. The capacity of a mask to enact its function depended on its state of cleanliness, which theoretically decreased while being worn or carried. In this way, the material capacity of a mask had the potential to change from a protective one to an infective one, while the owner/wearer could not be aware of this change. Such concerns were often not publicly debated, but rather found place in the washing and disposal practices of masking and the decisions of when to wash or bin.

Many of these supposedly transient things find themselves stuffed in a pocket coat or stashed at the bottom of a bag that is rarely used—crumpled but not quite ready to be binned. We encounter them when we decide to wear the coat again or reuse a bag. They are the material reminders of when we did not leave the home without a mask. Although facemasks are rarely worn in the UK now, we perhaps cannot bring ourselves to throw away the ones we find in drawers or pockets: they were once so important that their potency lives on. It reminds us that for a period of time facemasks became part of our essential items—kept alongside keys, phones, and wallets (Lupton et al., 2021). They were an element in the assemblage of things that we never left the house without, and now they are crumpled in pockets and drawers. They speak of the potential for this to happen again. Vanessa, one of the book's authors, observes that she has kept some masks in the hallway as if 'I don't fully believe that the pandemic is over, that I might still need to put on a mask when visiting a doctor'. The possibility of storing them away gained traction when the WHO pronounced on 5 May 2023 that Covid-19 is no longer a global health emergency, and led to the question of whether we *should* store them away and therefore move on from the pandemic. Putting the masks away would be a way to move on. One of the other authors, Leah, has put a face mask in her children's memory box along with a receipt from a Covid-19 test. The act of putting them in the memory box is a way of situating the pandemic in time, and also of moving on.

Materials have their own lifespans and afterlives (Kaiser & Smelik, 2020); thinking about masks and masking can mean looking back to where things come from, and how things were, as well as how things could be again. The divergent histories of different objects and indeed materials means that we can think about how these material relations change, but also our expectations and practices of masking change. In this regard, the relation to masks has an important temporal quality, generating a past of urgency and anxieties, creating a present lull where they are less visible, and speak to futures where they may be useful, needed, or mandated again. They relate to risks and freedoms, health and care. They conjure times when we could not visit our closest loved ones, yet were bound to many across the globe who shared experiences finding themselves in comparable situations and with similar concerns. Thinking about the materialities of masks in terms of their histories, presents, and future trajectories can thus produce insights into how people dealt with and lived the social changes and uncertainties of a pandemic.

Relationalities of Masks

The example given in the previous section of a face mask becoming an item of fancy dress for a ninja is one which shows the changing uses and relationalities of the face mask. For many, masks moved from being an essential item placed by the door with housekeys or in a handbag with everyday items, to stuffed in the pockets of a rarely used coat, or in the back of a drawer (Lupton et at., 2021). Masks are things that exist in relation to other things as well as *being* relations between heterogenous materials, which Bennett discusses as an assemblage (2010). Whilst in the main we have no challenges recognising something as a mask, we consider here that there is no isolated object "the mask" but instead it is itself relations between multiple material elements: breath, the skin, the virus, the materials we breathe through, and the materials of the ear hooks, to name a few.

A useful concept in thinking through material relationality is that of hybridity (Latour, 1993): materials or objects—technologies, people, animals, tables, masks—are not, ontologically speaking, separate entities but are heterogeneously connected to other entities that may be material, human, nonhuman, technological, or apparently found in nature. The notion of hybridity, then, conjures a world of interconnected entities rather than a world composed of separate entities and, importantly understands entities as products of their relations rather than relations as the product of entities. Relations are ontologically prior; objects are derivatives. It is then possible to follow the series of connections from masks to other entities—such as to scientific knowledge production about viral transmission, and materials on which infections can be spread. Masks are also connected to the materials that constitute them, and the manufacturing and logistics processes through which they are made and distributed.

But the relationality of masking can also be thought of in terms of how things mediate relations *between people*. Interactions are an extension of masking as a set of relations, as what is incorporated by these relations expands. There is a relation between different people wearing masks or not, and collectively a room of people wearing masks together can be a way to make manifest a shared position on the pandemic. The material relations of masking when considered in terms of interactions incorporate how people feel in the mask (discussed further below) as well as how the mask appears. Indeed, the visibility of the mask, as well as what it renders invisible is a key part of its materiality. As the virus itself is invisible and unseen, the visibility of the mask becomes significant as a way in which people make manifest their position in relation to it. As will be discussed further in Chap. 3, masks became a significant visual cue of how interactions might go or how they might be avoided, becoming very significant to judgement (moral and practical judgement alike: should I avoid talking to this person, or do I feel safe?). The relation of mask wearer to non-mask wearer is one then that can elicit awkwardness in the social encounter with someone you know, or a moral judgment in the case of strangers in a supermarket (see Chap. 4). The mask is highly visible, and this impacts how we negotiate interactions—is someone wearing a medical grade mask, is it only worn over their mouth? These questions are not ones we necessarily think through prior to the interaction, but rather we react by stepping back, or moving closer, or deciding to engage with someone.

Masks as relations then allows us to think about relations between people, as well as social relations more broadly. This can be the configuration of new relations as well as part of the exacerbation of existing divisions and inequalities. Inglis and Almila (2020), for example, highlight how black men in the US may be afraid to wear a mask in a shop as they are more likely to be presumed to be committing a robbery. We build on these ideas in the final section of this chapter to think through how the materiality of the masks connect to experiences of comfort and discomfort.

Comfort and Discomfort: Thinking Through Masking with Veiling

Feeling comfortable in clothing is to be physically and socially at ease, where clothing allows you to not feel self-conscious (Miller & Woodward, 2012). We can then consider a face mask to be comfortable when we feel at ease in it (see also Ahmed, 2014). The physical sensation of comfort may map on to the social or may feel out of synch, as we are wearing a facemask that is physically comfortable yet feel self-conscious due to the context. To be comfortable arises in part then from how one feels wearing the mask in the presence of others. As we move through different contexts and settings, feelings of comfort and discomfort shift depending upon where we are, who we see, and whether they are wearing a mask. Sara Ahmed (2014) expands comfort beyond the individual body and objects such as clothing to how bodies feel comfortable in public spaces. The masked face disrupts this sense of feeling at ease or comfortable as public spaces have typically been hostile to forms of masking and other face coverings. Ahmed notes that we do not tend to notice what is comfortable, unless this is disrupted and we come to feel discomfort where bodies feel out of place, awkward, and an 'acute awareness of the surface of one's body [...] when one cannot inhabit the social skin, which is shaped by some bodies, and not others' (Ahmed, 2014, p. 148). Masking positions bodies and people and can make them comfortable or ill at ease. For many people, masking for the first time in 2020 entailed novel feelings of discomfort in public spaces. But the materiality of masks also makes manifest existing feelings of marginality, discomfort, or social unease (Jenss & Hofmann, 2021). What Ahmed's writing points to is that many people already felt ill at ease and already subjected to a negative gaze in particular public spaces; encountering this for the first time when wearing a face mask highlights racialised privileges.

As discussed further in Chap. 3, the racialised nature of public spaces differentially shaped different groups' experiences of the public realm during the pandemic. The reasons for this are multiple, but it is particularly pertinent to consider how people who cover their face or head have been made to feel ill at ease prior to the considerable uptake of masking in public during the pandemic. Whilst there are clear connections between practices of face veiling and masks in terms of how covering the face impacts upon experiences and interactions, the differences also highlight important inequalities in terms of how people are seen. Many countries that have imposed public masking also have legislation that restricts the wearing of face veils, such as France and Austria (Inglis & Almila, 2020). Indeed, Inglis and Almila (2020) are not the only ones to point out the paradox that in some countries such as France and Austria, governments that had previously legislated a ban on Muslim women wearing a veil in public (often under the guise of concerns about security and capacities for interaction) put in place mask mandates during the Covid-19 pandemic. There are numerous examples of the banning of different forms of veiling, and the meanings associated with the veil are contextually specific. In the UK, on occasions where people had been asked to remove veils or where teachers lost their job due to wearing the niqab, public discourse explicitly framed this as an issue of communication, that verbal and visual communication are impeded (Lewis, 2015). The Islamic veil can thus be seen as 'semiotically overcharged' (Tarlo, 2007, p. 135), politicised, and hyper-visible in public discourse, while simultaneously women who veil are rendered invisible as they are objects of debate as veiled women become a sign of otherness (Bilge, 2010; Lewis, 2015).

In her anthropological account of the hijab in London, Tarlo (2007) centres the agency of the hijab (Tarlo, 2007) as it both transforms women's sense of themselves but also how they relate to other people and the social spaces and environment around them. Tarlo discusses the "resonances" of the veil as a way to connect how people experience and live the multiple meanings the veil has; these are positive (notions of modesty, privacy) and negative (specific encounters with people, public links to terrorism and oppression). These negative resonances are ones which those who veil have to negotiate and live with. This approach is instructive to how we can think through masks in centring the materiality of the mask, the connotations and "resonances" it may have, and how people negotiate these meanings through experiences of wearing it. We have already discussed the ways in which the visibility of the mask (what type or the wearing of it at all) impacts upon how people relate to each other. But the mask has also become politically hyper-visible in public discourse and discussions (see Lewis, 2015 on hyper-visibility and politicisation of veiling). Just as Tarlo notes for the veil that the veil may also make someone 'visible as Muslim' (2007, p. 132), the facemask (or absence thereof) came to be an identifier of a person's position towards the pandemic and its restrictions. Yet, as discussed in Chaps. 3 and 4, this also yielded the potential for people's positions to be "misidentified", as those who were exempt from masking often found themselves subject to expressive challenges and even abuse (Hanna et al., 2022).

Thinking about masks in terms of comfort encompasses both the visibilities of the masked person as well as how a person feels. Masking came to present a tangible means through which people worked out who they were, how they felt about the pandemic, and what they thought about masking in certain circumstances, as they made decisions over masking in different social settings and assessed the decisions of others. Writing about veiling, Unal (2023) notes that this sense of working out who we are includes people's anxieties and vulnerabilities. Gökarıksel and Secor (2020) write about the assemblages of veiling as a way to step back from thinking about what the veil "means", and instead think about what it does: for example, how does veiling impact upon how people interact or form their sense of self. They discuss specific effects in relation to the veil, including the struggles and dilemmas veiling creates, as well as what veiling makes possible. Wearing the veil every day, for example, allows the ongoing cultivation and ongoing "doing" of being a pious Muslim woman. This routine wearing is thus also orienting a person towards an ideal. This echoes with our discussion of masking in terms of comfort/discomfort and the relations between routine wearing and feelings of self-consciousness. Wearing a mask may allow people to feel they are behaving in a moral and reasonable fashion, as the mask allows them to orient themselves towards this ideal (see Chap. 4). The mask also orients how others behave to us, as for example the unmasked may lead us to step back or to cross the road. The mask then is a route through which we orient our own and other behaviours, as well as how we cultivate our sense of who we are in a pandemic. These points open up themes that are explored in more depth in the next two chapters.

Conclusion

This chapter began by exploring and reinterpreting masks through the lens of multiple materialities. We used this to show that masks are multiple in practice, not just in moments of use, but in how they are made, stored, kept, styled, and disposed of. We explored the material agencies of masks, focusing on the ways they change bodily sensations and affect. Shifting increasingly towards a relational vocabulary, we showed how masks have an ever-changing presence and create new signals for people in different contexts. The materiality and meanings of masks emerge simultaneously through a physical-interpretive negotiation, producing masks as they should be worn, wearers and non-wearers, and the meanings associated with each. Focusing on masks also helps explore the relation of practice, physicality, and time. The temporalities of masking are deeply entwined with affect—how we feel about pandemic's past, present, and future, and what masks meant and mean, especially now many of them are hidden away, scrunched up, but still potent in their capacities and meanings.

Finally, we showed how the practices of masking are varied, and produce different discomforts for different reasons, a theme explored further throughout the book. These discussions on material performativity and relationality work in parallel with Chaps. 3 and 4, where we explore interactions in public and the moralities of masks.

References

Ahmed, S. (2014). *Cultural politics of emotion*. Edinburgh University Press.

Bennett, J. (2010). *Vibrant matter: A political ecology of things*. Duke University Press.

Bilge, S. (2010). Beyond subordination vs. resistance: An intersectional approach to the agency of veiled Muslim women. *Journal of Intercultural Studies, 31*(1), 9–28.

Boscagli, M. (2014). *Stuff theory: Everyday objects and radical materialism*. Bloomsbury.

Coole, D., & Frost, S. (Eds.). (2010). *New materialisms: Ontology, agency, and politics*. Duke University Press.

Crandall, C. S., Bahns, A. J., & Gillath, O. (2022). Do masks affect social interaction? *Journal of Applied Social Psychology, 52*(12), 1172–1178.

Gell, A. (1998). *Art and agency: An anthropological theory*. Clarendon Press.

Gökarıksel, B., & Secor, A. J. (2020). Beyond the symbolism of the headscarf: The assemblage of veiling and the headscarf as a thing. *The Wiley Blackwell Companion to Religion and Materiality*, 328–340.

Hanna, E., Martin, G., Campbell, A., Connolly, P., Fearon, K., & Markham, S. (2022). Experiences of face mask use during the COVID-19 pandemic: A qualitative study. *Sociology of Health & Illness, 44*(9), 1481–1499.

Haraway, D. J. (1985). A cyborg manifesto. Technology and socialist feminism in the late twentieth century. *Simians, Cyborgs and Women. The Reinvention of Nature*, 149–181.

Inglis, D., & Almila, A.-M. (2020). Un-Masking the mask: Developing the sociology of facial politics in pandemic times and after. *SocietàMutamentoPolitica, 11*(21), 251–257.

Jenss, H., & Hofmann, V. (Eds.). (2021). *Fashion and materiality: Cultural practices in global contexts*. Bloomsbury Publishing.

Kaiser, S. B., & Smelik, A. (2020). Materials and materialities: Viral and sheep-ish encounters with fashion. *Critical Studies in Fashion & Beauty, 11*(1), 9–19.

Keough, S. B. (2021). Masks and materiality in the era of COVID-19. *Geographical Review, 111*(4), 558–570.

Knorr Cetina, K. (2001). Objectual practice. In T. Schatzki, K. Knorr Cetina, & E. von Savigny (Eds.), *The practice turn in contemporary theory* (pp. 184–197). Routledge.

Latour, B. (1993). *We have never been modern*. Harvard University Press.

Law, J. (2002). *Aircraft stories: Decentering the object in technoscience*. Duke University Press.

Lewis, R. (2015). Uncovering modesty: Dejabis and dewigies expanding the parameters of the modest fashion blogosphere. *Fashion Theory, 19*(2), 243–269.

Lupton, D. et al. (2021). *The face mask in COVID times: A sociomaterial analysis*. De Gruyter.

Miller, D. (1997). *Material culture and mass consumerism*. John Wiley & Sons.

Miller, D. (2005). Materiality: An introduction. *Materiality, 1*, 1–50.

Miller, D., & Woodward, S. (2007). Manifesto for a study of denim. *Social Anthropology/Anthropologie Sociale, 15*(3), 335–351.

Miller, D., & Woodward, S. (2012). *Blue jeans: The art of the ordinary*. University of California Press.

Mol, A. (2002). *The body multiple: Ontology in medical practice*. Duke University.

Pickering, A. (1995). *The mangle of practice: Time, agency, and science*. University of Chicago Press.

Serres, M. (1982). *The parasite* (L. R. Schehr, Trans.). Johns Hopkins University Press.

Sharma, S. K., Mishra, M., & Mudgal, S. K. (2020). Efficacy of cloth face mask in prevention of novel coronavirus infection transmission: A systematic review and meta-analysis. *Journal of Education and Health Promotion, 9*, 192.

Smelik, A. (2018). New materialism: A theoretical framework for fashion in the age of technological innovation. *International Journal of Fashion Studies, 5*(1), 33–54.

St. Pierre, E. A., Jackson, A. Y., & Mazzei, L. A. (2016). New empiricisms and new materialisms: Conditions for new inquiry. *Cultural Studies? Critical Methodologies, 16*(2), 99–110.

Tarlo, E. (2007). Hijab in London: Metamorphosis, resonance and effects. *Journal of Material Culture, 2*(2), 131–156.

Unal, D. (2023). Navigating stigma through refashioning islamic veiling: Muslim women's sartorial de-stigmatization strategies in contemporary united states. *Fashion Theory*, 1–25.

CHAPTER 3

Masking and the (Re)making of the Public Realm

Abstract This chapter explores masks as mediating interactions between strangers and acquaintances during the height of the pandemic. We are particularly interested in the interactional discomfort and negotiations that ensued as masking unsettled unwritten rules of co-mingling. This entailed both visible and measurable adjustments to frequency and length of interactions but also the more intangible dimension of how people experienced interactions that were no longer as predictable as they had been pre-pandemic. To address these questions, we draw from Goffman's iconic work on how public order is regulated in face-to-face interaction. Our analysis leads us to critically examine the Eurocentric readings of the significance of "face" in interactions, as well as how these have informed academic research on the topic of masking. We also draw from a recent body of work exploring disruptions as essential to public order to explore the vital role played by interactional discomfort as people figured out what the new rules of interaction were. In doing so, we pay attention to how people's experiences were shaped by underlying power inequalities and the role that trust and solidarity played in constituting "safe" stranger interactions.

Keywords Masks • Public realm • Relational interaction • Disruption • Goffman • Face • Inequality

O. Abbott et al., *Masking in the Pandemic*, Consumption and Public Life, https://doi.org/10.1007/978-3-031-45781-4_3

Introduction

This chapter builds on the discussions in Chap. 2 which, drawing from new materialist approaches, presented masks as material things that mediate relations between people. We now move on to explore in more depth the nature of masked interactions. During the height of the Covid-19 pandemic, masking was, in the main, mandatory in public settings. This is why our focus lies on relations in public and on the effect that the rapid emergence and visible proliferation of masking had on the character of interactions that took place in public settings such as streets, shops, and parks. If we understand the public realm as constituted through interactions, then masking was part of the constitution of that public realm during the height of the pandemic. The introduction of masking in countries such as the UK where the use of masks had hitherto been rare can be seen as a natural "breaching experiment" (Garfinkel, 1967; Scambler, 2020) that unsettled unwritten rules of co-mingling. While this chapter explores what such a breach meant for the nature of interactions, in Chap. 4 we examine the moral contestations that it also entailed and how these were worked out in everyday interactions.

As sociologists we are interested in the negotiations—both silent and vociferous—as well as interactional discomfort that such a disturbance gave rise to. We propose that paying attention to the interactional uncertainty and discomfort and even conflict that the introduction of masking led to brings to light in a heightened fashion the work that is involved in (re)making the public realm. To make sense of this process, we draw from Goffman's (1963, 1967, 1971) iconic work on how public order is regulated in face-to-face interaction, as well as from a recent body of work exploring disruptions as an essential part of this order (Tavory, 2018; Tavory & Fine, 2020). Building on the discussions in Chap. 2 about how masking cannot be understood divorced from existing social divisions and inequalities, we are attuned to the fact that a person's choice to mask or not in public was read differently depending on their age, gender, and ethnicity. This meant that people encountered different public realms. Furthermore, the visible materiality of masks which cover the lower part of the face leads us to critically examine Eurocentric readings of the significance of "face" in face-to-face interactions which have informed academic research on the topic of masking.

Setting the Scene: Masks in Interaction

Masking, novel as it was in most Westernised countries, sparked considerable interest among researchers during the height of the Covid-19 pandemic. Much of the research on masking and social interactions was conducted by social psychologists and behavioural scientists, who were mainly focused on studying emotion recognition in experimental situations. The results were mixed. Some argued that mask wearing impedes emotion recognition, which in turn can make it more difficult for people to form a connection with each other (Carbon, 2020; Chester et al., 2023; Grundmann et al., 2021) while others found that the impact of masks is minimal (Calbi et al., 2021; Ruba & Pollak, 2020). What is interesting to note about this body of research is the significance that is accorded to facial cues in interaction among strangers such as stretching, parting, or thinning one's lips, wrinkling one's nose, and dropping one's jaw (Mheidly et al., 2020). Grundmann et al. (2021) argue that because masks occlude such facial cues, which strangers rely on to communicate predictability to each other, masking has a negative impact on the tone of interactions among strangers, making it harder to build trust and a sense of closeness. In our own observations, we noted the difficulties we had in communicating with others in the first months of masking:

> *Vanessa (January 2021): One of my first masked interactions was with my GP. Every other sentence, I had to say 'Sorry, I didn't catch that'. With only his eyes visible, his speech was a muffled jumble of words that I couldn't begin to decipher. This was in the summer of 2020, when it was still a distinct possibility that we would be teaching on campus in masks—I was dreading the thought. These past weeks, as I've been listening to podcasts about the insurrection on the Capitol in Washington DC, I've become accustomed to hearing political speeches delivered in Congress through masks (which are not worn by MPs in parliament in the UK). Maybe masked teaching might be possible, though we won't always have the benefit of a microphone.*

Muffled speech and the loss of facial expressions in masked communication were likely to have been noticed by many people, but perhaps particularly by those with hearing impairments, who were among those most likely to have experienced an increased sense of isolation and loneliness during the pandemic (Homans & Vroegop, 2021). Collins (2020) observed that one way for people to counteract the muffling effects of face masks on speech was to raise their voices, which could be misunderstood as a sign of annoyance or anger. This is why, masked interaction, even when ostensibly civil, 'takes its toll' (Collins, 2020, p. 486).

Crandall et al.'s (2022) study, conducted before the pandemic among American college students to assess the impact that covering one's face has on interactions among strangers, is rare in that it focuses on how masking influences how people feel about social interactions. The study participants were asked to approach someone in a lecture hall and engage them in conversation. Half of the participants were wearing a mask, hat, and sunglasses, while the other half were without any face apparel. Both parties were then asked to rate how they felt about the interaction. Crandall et al. found that mask wearing had no discernible effect on the perceived quality of these stranger interactions: 'there was no loss of friendliness, appeal, authenticity, similarity, or comfort in the activity' (p. 1176). One reason for this, they say, is that interaction participants made use of a host of non-facial cues to make sense of the other person. These include posture, gestures, verbal and paralinguistic cues, as well as what the person is wearing. Carbon (2020) and Ruba and Pollak (2020) similarly point out that people have many tools at their disposal to convey emotions and are likely to use these in an enhanced manner to counteract the effects of masking. Crandall et al. caveat their findings by noting that these were derived at a time when mask wearing did not yet denote a particular political attitude. In contrast, during the Covid-19 pandemic, 'the meaning of wearing masks had become divisive and politically tinged' in many countries (p. 1176). We explore the political polarisation that occurred around masking, and its moral consequences, in Chap. 4.

As we have discussed in Chap. 2, a mask is thus not just a piece of cloth but is imbued with meaning, partly derived from being part of an assemblage of things, people, and practices. Collins (2020) observed an increase in public solidarity at the beginning of the pandemic in suburban America, evident in a sharp rise in the number of friendly fleeting interactions as (mostly masked) people acknowledged and made way for others with whom their paths crossed. Collins proposes that in the context of a shared threat (of the novel coronavirus), masking was a way for people to signal to others that they were united in the fight against a common enemy. But this kind of solidarity was short-lived. Collins notes that the frequency of friendly greetings dropped off after a couple of months, while the number of masked people also declined in public spaces where mask wearing was not enforced.

The meanings attached to masks and to those wearing them also changed through the different stages of the pandemic. As we explore in more depth in Chap. 4, these meanings had moral undertones. Van Gorp (2021, p. 126) observed in Belgium that 'the individuals who wore masks in supermarkets at the beginning of the pandemic were viewed with suspicion, possibly even more than those who were hoarding'. Once mask wearing had become ubiquitous, it was those who did *not* wear a mask who came under suspicion of not "doing their bit" to curb Covid-19 infection rates (Hanna et al., 2022). This was in a context where some governments were promoting masking as crucial for protecting the health of self and others. People who did not wear masks could be judged by others as behaving in an idiotic and selfish manner (Hanna et al., 2022). And those who were exempt from wearing a mask could experience anxiety when entering public spaces, fearing the judgement of others and anticipating conflict. Hanna et al. (2022) point out that the flip side of evoking a sense of solidarity around mask wearing as an altruistic act to protect others is that those who cannot wear masks risk being othered, stigmatised and marginalised, many of whom are already othered and marginalised due to disability or ethnicity.

But, when considering the impact of masking on social interactions in public, masking in itself does not tell the full story. Mask mandates were in many countries introduced in conjunction with social distancing measures, stay-at-home orders, and the closure of public spaces such as cafes, shops, and even playgrounds. As discussed in Chap. 2, masks (or the lack of one) acted as a material and visual reminder of the Covid-19 virus and of the requirement to socially distance oneself from others. In doing so, masks "dramatized" the space between people (Inglis & Almila, 2020, p. 255; Harms, 2020). Indeed, Inglis and Almila propose that '[t]he mask is pre-eminently a device aimed at the *re-engineering of space and spatial relations*' (2020, p. 255, emphasis in original). In addition, masking became a visible feature in public at a time when fears around Covid-19 were high because viral spread, containment, and treatment were still poorly understood. At the beginning of the pandemic, it was unclear 'how space should be used such that it will not negatively impact the health of oneself or others' (James, 2020, p. 187). It is our contention that masks became a visible and tangible vector that symbolised risk of infection and the accompanying fear of illness, as well as the different political meanings attached to masking. As a result, masking became the focus of heated disagreements over what the right course of action was in this novel situation. We explore these questions in more depth in Chap. 4.

The research on the impact of masking and other pandemic measures on social interactions in public spaces was mostly interested in the visible and measurable, namely, reduced emotion recognition and attitudes towards masking, as discussed above, and levels of interaction in public spaces (e.g. Askarizad et al., 2021; Finlay et al., 2022; Mehta, 2020; Zetterberg et al., 2021). We argue that beyond this, in contexts where masking was a novel practice, it offers the opportunity to train our sociological gaze on the question of how social interaction orders are (re)negotiated.

Disrupting Unwritten Rules of Interaction

The rapid emergence of masks in Western contexts made visible the fact that the unwritten rules of public interaction are never set but instead negotiated in an ongoing fashion. To make sense of how social change is negotiated at the micro-level of interaction, we draw from Goffman's work on how public order is regulated in face-to-face interaction and the patterned behaviour that results (Goffman, 1963, 1967, 1971). Goffman explored sedimented and taken-for-granted interactions, meaning that he was less concerned with the process whereby social order and rules of interaction become established. Whereas the unwritten rules of interaction studied by Goffman (1971) such as "civil inattention"—which entails affording other people the civility of acknowledging their presence while helping them to protect their sense of privacy by not directing undue attention towards them—are so deeply embedded as to be second nature and therefore not usually noticed, there were no sedimented patterns of interaction around wearing masks. As a consequence, people had to make on-the-spot decisions about how to interact with each other. Our interest lies in understanding what happens when established rules of engagement are no longer sufficient and interactions do not have a routine pattern. This led to the invention of new rituals, such as the friendly waves and hellos that accompanied people's often clumsy efforts to adhere to social distancing, as observed by Collins (2020). Collins interprets these rituals as attempts to repair the act of visibly stepping away from people, which previously would have been interpreted as a breach of civil inattention.

Another interesting feature of the pandemic was that the new public realm never fully settled into an established routine because rules and practices had to constantly adapt to changing circumstances, as perfectly illustrated by an episode of the Netflix series *Love Life*:

Vanessa (March 2023): Last night I watched an episode of an American series that is set in the spring of 2020. The episode captures well the awkwardness of social interactions where both parties take a second's pause as they try to communicate with each other how to proceed and where movements are hesitant and commented upon verbally. In one scene, the main character Marcus cycles through the eerily empty streets of New York to visit his sister's flat. She opens the door, wearing a mask, and backs away several steps into the flat with her hands up, palms facing Marcus. He does a little jig on the spot, waiting for his sister to move far enough away before he enters. Haltingly, standing far apart from each other, they cross their arms in front of themselves in a hugging motion. He laughs nervously, saying 'Air hug' and she repeats 'Air hug, air hug', while the sister's partner comments 'I'm sorry we can't hug you'. In a later scene, at his sister's wedding, Marcus approaches her and asks, 'We doing the... [motioning a hug with his arms]?', to which she responds 'We might as well', before they lean in to hug each other.

Sikka (2021, p. 8) argues that masking led to a 'transformation in how we relate to each other' because it disrupted the hitherto ordinary sense of relationality between self and Other. As already indicated by the literature reviewed above, people who had previously relied on verbal communication, aided by facial expressions, were likely to find that masks, which cover the lower part of the face and muffle speech, impeded their ability to convey and understand meaning and emotions in interaction (Collins, 2020). This was of course not the case for everyone, as for example people with facial paralysis and those hard of hearing had to find solutions to such issues already before the pandemic (Bogart, 2021). In our own lives, we observed that masking made hitherto taken-for-granted interactions in public awkward to the point that it was difficult to get them "right", as noted by Sophie about encounters with other parents at the school gate:

Sophie (February, 2021): My main encounter with public spaces and other people is dropping my children off at school. I do not wear a mask from the house, but put it on on the street the school is located. There are a number of people I know enough to smile at or say hello to. Smiling is obviously not an option when masked, nor is a quiet hello and even a slight nod of the head feels not quite enough without an accompanying smile. We are left either with a loud hello which feels too much, a slightly awkward look at someone, or looking at the floor or into the distance.

It is perhaps such fleeting encounters with acquaintances that were most transformed because the customary quick hello became difficult to perform with ease and stopping to verbally negotiate a new style of greeting probably felt inappropriate or "too much". These encounters were perhaps even more awkward when one party was masked and the other not. Some might have wished to keep such interactions brief because the mask reminded them of the potential presence of a highly transmissible virus, especially if the other person was not wearing a mask. The physical discomfort of wearing a mask (discussed in Chap. 2) and the way masks impede communication probably encouraged people to move along without stopping to chat to someone as they might have pre-pandemic. The loss of such fleeting interactions is significant because they offer opportunities for what in the UK is known as "banter", which, when done appropriately, is known to increase a sense of solidarity (Culpeper, 1996).

But masks should not be viewed purely as having an inhibiting effect on social interaction in public. It is important to consider not just the materiality of the mask and how it might impede "normal" conversation. Indeed, we observed that over time, masked conversations became easier to conduct. Another important feature that impacted how people felt about masked interactions was that (not) wearing a mask signalled to others one's (moral) attitude towards the pandemic and pandemic measures. As we go on to discuss in Chap. 4, it was in interaction that people were jointly working out a new moral order, and in doing so, influencing each other's thinking and future behaviour. Masking could become a way of building trust between like-minded people who either felt that the pandemic measures were an overreaction or that adhering to mask mandates was a way to "do one's bit" to keep others safe. Sophie's example below of how masking facilitated rather than hindered encounters between people is a perfect example of the pandemic solidarity that Collins (2020) observed in his neighbourhood:

> *Sophie (February, 2021): More recently, with the new variant of the virus there has been more masking of parents at the school gates, and one close friend always wears a mask as we stand apart but are able to chat. I am no longer self-conscious about the mask and wearing it; whilst conversation is a little different this becomes a new normal social interaction. This relates to the ways in which we are both wearing masks, and this indicates mutual respect of each other, as well that we are taking the pandemic seriously. When I arrive early in the playground I put the mask in my pocket as there is no one about, and seeing a friend*

walk over I put it on for the encounter—she does the same. Rather than masking inhibiting interactions instead in this instance it enables and allows it.

In the example above, donning a mask acts as a signal to begin a conversation. A further potentially positive effect of masking, according to Perini and Sciara (2022), is that the greater sense of anonymity afforded by a mask can reduce self-awareness, thus encouraging greater spontaneity in interaction with strangers. Such spontaneity can of course also have negative consequences, as when people feel less inhibited to hurl abuse at a passer-by. It is worth noting that such reduced self-awareness is less likely to be afforded to racialised minorities wearing masks, as we discuss below.

The above discussion indicates that when masking mandates were in place and masking was a widespread practice, many people experienced that a relatively high proportion of their daily interactions flowed less "naturally". Long et al. (2022, p. 129) propose that as rates of Covid-19 infection waxed and waned and pandemic restrictions were lifted, then reinstated, then lifted again, and as knowledge about how the virus was transmitted improved, negotiating the ensuing ever-changing norms of social interaction required 'intense cognitive effort'. For example, and as we also have noted above, Long et al. observed that people were uncertain about 'how to bring closure to an in-person interaction or convey warmth' (Long et al., 2022, p. 129). The destabilising effect that the pandemic had on established 'scripted ways of interacting' was particularly difficult for those 'who already struggled to encode and decode interactions with others', such as those who are deaf or people on the autism spectrum. These difficulties, Long et al. (2022, p. 129) say, were 'intensified by mask wearing'.

The Two Sides of Disruption

We now move on to consider the ways in which people can respond to a situation when social interaction does not follow a familiar pattern. One possible reaction to such interactional uncertainty is 'the challenge, by which participants take on the responsibility of calling attention to the misconduct' (Goffman, 1967, p. 20). James (2020) observed that during the pandemic, people who disregarded social distancing measures and did not wear masks were mostly challenged through subtle cues such as coughing and shuffling. But, in an atmosphere where masking became a politically polarising practice that was hotly debated (Bhasin et al., 2020), the wearing or not wearing of a mask could also lead to a person becoming the target of intense scrutiny, impoliteness, and even aggression. Masks thus operated as objects that highlighted old and new boundaries of social cohesion and hierarchy (Pfaller, 2020). Indeed, as Covid-19 rates began to rise, the “stranger” gained new negative undertones as a potential source of infection (Iranmanesh & Alpar Atun, 2021). As we discuss below, it was particularly racialised minorities who became targets of suspicion in majority white countries in the Global North.

Social and print media abounded with reports of verbal and sometimes physical aggression between people sparked by the wearing of a mask or the absence of one. These interactions were examples of an ‘aggressive use of face-work’, the purpose of which is not ‘mutual considerateness’ but to score points against an adversary (Goffman, 1967: 24). Extreme disagreements over masking are examples of conflicts where the parties ‘do not necessarily share beliefs, frequently do not accept the validity of one another’s intention, and often disagree even about the descriptions that people offer for acts’ (Alexander, 2004, p. 527, quoted in Horgan, 2020, p. 124). These disruptions that masking caused mattered because ‘interactional norms are key relational mechanisms which build trust, belonging and identity within and across groups in a system’ (Long et al., 2022, p. 129). The shared use of public space is predicated on this sense of ‘trust and shared interest’ (James, 2020, p. 188). James argues that building such trust became difficult as levels of interaction reduced. Indeed, levels of social trust, that is, a general sense of trust in other people, were found to have fallen in the early phases of the pandemic (Lo Iacono et al., 2021).

It is, however, worth querying whether all and any disruptions to social interaction weaken trust. Tavory and Fine (2020) critique microsociology for its overwhelming focus on alignment and consensus and argue against the commonly held notion that disruptions to interactional harmony are necessarily something to be overcome or a sign of failure. In fact, completely smooth interactions can feel ‘unnerving’ and ‘create problems of intersubjectivity’, while it is thanks to the ‘back and forth between moments of smoothness and disruption’ that actors are able to (re)calibrate the ‘definition of the situation’ (Tavory, 2018, p. 125). Therefore, instead of focusing on intersubjectivity and the construction of social order, as is more common, Tavory and Fine (2020, p. 327) analyse disruption as ‘essential to any interactional order’ and as routinely managed in interaction. A focus on ‘the choreography of alignment and disruption’ allows us to see how new modes of ‘social coordination’ are created

(p. 366). In other words, disruptions can act as a resource in interaction, as exemplified by Collins's (2020) observation of how attempts to repair a situation can lead to the invention of new rituals, such as the elbow bumps and 'air hugs' that people adopted as a form of greeting during the pandemic. We propose that interactional uncertainty, discomfort, and even conflict that the introduction of masking led to were generative of the new social order in the context of pandemic measures.

Ambiguity in Interaction

There was no absolute shift to masking, and the ambiguities of masking practices laid bare the fact that people are rarely equipped with a clear set of rules of interaction but must instead always employ a degree of creativity in interpreting what they think is "the done thing" (Drury & Stokoe, 2022; Katila et al., 2020). In some public spaces, the expectations around masking practices were ambiguous, giving rise to interactional uncertainty:

> *Owen (December 2020): Particularly at the start, I was unsure (and still am unsure) exactly when I should be wearing a mask in public. I know I have to wear it on a train and nearly always inside, but do I need it if I sit with a friend in the park or as I walk through the corridors of my apartment building (with most people not wearing masks in these cases)? This then feeds into interactional and contextual indeterminacy: I'm outside, but several other people around me are wearing a mask, should I be wearing a mask?*

Owen indicates above that even in spaces where the rules were clear, such as in the UK on the streets, where masks were never mandated and where most people did not wear a mask, people had to make situation-specific decisions about whether it would in fact be considerate to wear one. Encounters in these open spaces became, for some, less straightforward during the pandemic. Bumping into a neighbour or casual acquaintance, some might not have felt comfortable to pause to chat, or they might have consciously moved slightly further away from each other in order to do this. Indeed, Mehta (2020) observed in his neighbourhood in Cincinnati that social interaction regularly took place between acquaintances and strangers at a greater distance than before. He noted that it was common to see friends walking down a street six feet apart or neighbours chatting to each other similarly distanced, comfortable with this new sociable space that would have felt awkward before the pandemic.

Even in spaces where mask mandates were in effect, masking practices varied. Some people always wore a mask, some did so in a half-masked way and others not at all. This made apparent that not everybody follows the same unwritten rules. In addition, the unwritten rules varied across different types of public space. What further complicated matters was that in any one space, different people might have been subject to varying rules of masking or could interpret these differently, or a person's masking practices could shift from day to day, as Rob observed at his son's nursery:

> *Rob (February, 2021): Walking up to nursery in the morning and afternoon, masks are visible. Other parents in various states of masking are both approaching and returning from the school gate. I usually carry my mask in my pocket and don it at the gate. It's mandatory on the schoolgrounds despite being outside and easy to stay away from others. Thus, there's transition to interact with a public object (school/nursery), in which parents are masking but most school staff are not. Unless they are meeting parents. Which is odd.*
>
> *When I arrive with my son, I squat, pull down my mask and we kiss each other, bye-bye. He runs in the door, under the arm of the nursery teacher. She wasn't masked today. Things I half notice. Not sure if she's masking less, or if it was just once. If she hasn't seen, she asks, 'Have you kissed daddy?', condoning my momentary unmasking.*

Interpretations of where one should and should not mask varied not merely across different types of space, but also according to the type of relationship and interaction involved. Rob observed that unmasking could denote closeness in a relationship, conveying a sense of trust:

> *Rob (February, 2021): My son has a current good friend at nursery and the two of them have taken to walking home together; our house first. His friend "drops him off". This means walking with his friend's family, too—sometimes one parent, or both and baby sister in a pushchair. Obviously (is it, obvious?), the children don't need to wear masks, and have been together and touching each other all day—my son kisses his friend goodbye every day, too—so we are in a* de facto *bubble. Or so we think. The parents are sort of moving from acquaintances, parents of a nursery-mate, to sort-of friends. Masking seems to indicate this—I noticed the mum taking her mask off shortly after I had as we left school and we all walked down the street. I stayed a greater distance than I used to before masking was a thing, but there's something inviting, relaxing, disarming about unmasking. A handshake of sorts.*

Not only did mask mandates change interactions in the public realm, but they also unsettled the hitherto assumed relationship between the private and the public spheres. It was at the threshold of the home where people entered the renegotiated public realm, arguably in a more heightened fashion than before. The most obvious example of this is the doorstep encounters with delivery drivers that became a regular feature in many people's lives as they ordered food and other items to be delivered to their homes:

> *Sophie (February, 2021): I get a vegetable box delivered every two weeks and the delivery man always wears a mask, rings the doorbell and walks back to his van; however, the retuning of the empty box to him necessitates more of an encounter. When he sees we are wearing a mask, he visibly relaxes as we hold out the box and he takes it.*

As Sophie's account attests, these hitherto ordinary encounters could be replete with anxieties, and significantly more so for those who were clinically vulnerable. The act of masking in such situations was an indicator of caring about the other person's health and showing respect to those whose work brought them into frequent contact with others. It is important to keep in mind the underpinning social inequalities which meant that many delivery drivers, as well as other service industry workers, were on minimum wage and precarious contracts, and therefore had little choice but to go out to work and thus expose themselves to a higher risk of catching Covid-19 (Inglis & Almila, 2020).

Transitions across different types of space and interaction, the ambiguities involved in making decisions about masking and how people attended to and marked public-private thresholds, are an important locus of attention as they speak to the complexities of the rules of interaction and the need to creatively interpret them. Masking was also a practice that could trouble and even change the distinction between public and private, at the same time making more noticeable the threshold between the two types of space.

"Face"—Literal or Symbolic?

Central to Goffman's work and much of the research published on the impact of masking on social interaction is the notion of "face". When individuals 'come into one another's immediate presence', they 'inevitably engage one another in communication of a sort', whether verbal or non-verbal (Goffman, 1963, p. 33). Goffman emphasised the role played by facial expressions in facilitating interaction, signalling intentions, the performance of roles, and displaying a face that is appropriate to the situation. Bourdieu (1992, pp. 80–81) encapsulated this as 'the art of playing on the equivocations, innuendos and unspoken implications of gestural or verbal symbolism' that is involved in even the most ritual of interactions. Owen noted how difficult it became, while wearing a mask, to display appropriate face and to convey the kind of emotion that would be fitting to a situation or that would contribute to a smooth interaction:

> *Owen (February, 2021): Displaying appropriate face becomes challenging. While wearing a mask to my grandad's funeral, I found myself wondering if the top half of my face looked appropriately solemn. I've found that role-fulfilling interactions, e.g. customer-cashier in a shop, became more mechanical and less endearing. Without being able to smile politely (the impression I want to "give") I sometimes wonder if I now come across as quite aloof (the impression I maybe "give off").*

Because of the unfamiliarity of mask wearing, it was no doubt common to be uncertain about what it was to be "in face", "in the wrong face", and "out of face" or whether one had "saved face" or "lost face" (see Goffman, 1967). It was also unclear how the situation could be repaired through tacit cooperation to help save each other's face.

Interactions are calibrated and managed through minute expressions and gestures to which people are intricately attuned. Changes of expression signal that we are joking or listening intently, or that we find dis/agreeable the line of conversation our interlocutor has embarked upon. These small gestures provide a mechanism through which the in situ 'correcting, sanctioning, criticizing [and] approving' of others occurs (Frega, 2015, p. 6). Depending on how successful this facial engagement is between strangers, it can 'either help start a conversation and friendly interpersonal interaction or, alternatively, invoke fear or aggression' (Jasiński, 2020, p. 5). According to Goffman (1967), people are so habituated into reading these expressive cues that they largely enact and respond to them without (much) conscious thought. Deliberative consciousness arises when stumbling blocks are encountered—a joke not landing as intended, being unsure of what the other person meant or why they changed their tone (Joas, 1990). As discussed above, masking can easily present such a stumbling block because masks can impede our ability to read 'interpersonal signals' (Jasiński, 2020, p. 5). It is perhaps not surprising that masked interactions were something that people at times wished to avoid. As Owen noted in February 2021, '*I've had a few occasions where I've favoured an awkward wave rather than going over to speak to someone I know fairly well if I see them in the street*'.

Our discussion so far has taken "face" at face value (no pun intended). This is because we have engaged with Eurocentric thought which assumes that "normal" social interaction and interpersonal communication takes place between two people whose faces are visible to each other. In many Western cultures, covering one's face has traditionally been considered a marker of cultural "otherness", as in the case of Muslim women who veil, as discussed in Chap. 2, or as a potential sign of criminality, where the mask is used to hide a person's identity (Moors, 2009; Patton, 2014).

Patton's (2014) paper analysing the public discourses in France in relation to the 2011 law banning the use of the face veil in public settings provides an alternative conceptualisation of "face". She notes that the report commissioned by the French government ahead of the change in legislation made several references to the French philosopher Emmanuel Levinas's work on the face. The report argues that ethical relations between citizens are possible only if they can see each other's literal faces. This has since become a common place argument in French public debate about veiling. Patton (2014, p. 194) argues that the reading of Levinas in this report is 'a gross misrepresentation'. On the contrary, she points out, Levinas's argument is that the face is not reducible to its 'plastic form' and that consequently, the face 'is not something I can visually apprehend' (p. 192). Indeed, Levinas was, according to Patton, critical of the narrow focus on visual perception, instead emphasising the importance of the other senses in human interaction. If the face is 'not a collection of physical features' and 'not bound to the realm of visual perception' but something whose 'meaning overflows its material presence', it is not something that can be concealed by a piece of fabric such as the veil or the face mask (p. 192). Instead, the face is 'the "living presence" of another person' (p. 193, 194). Levinas work can in other words *not* be used to argue, as the French government's report on veiling does, that ethical comportment requires seeing the literal face of the other.

Patton (2014) also brings to the fore the role of visual consumption of the Other in colonial relations, where the Other was reduced to an object of the colonial gaze. A legacy of this colonial gaze is the way in which non-Muslims are 'accustomed to drawing the Other into the familiar play of the Same' on the basis of the 'visibility of the Other's physical face' (p.195). In other words, the only way in which Westerners feel they can find some similarity with the Other is if they see their faces. Deleuze and Guattari (1987) have argued that the face has become overcoded in Western cultures, meaning that faces have come to be seen as separate from their bodily context and have been made crucial to understanding people and their biographies, intentions, and emotions. The face is privileged over other bodily expressions and facial understandings are lent weight and certainty. Patton (2014) argues that when Muslim women cover their faces with the veil, many non-Muslims feel affronted by the perceived lack of reciprocity. For them, the relationship that ensues is unequal because they feel they are the weaker party if their interlocutor can see their face but not vice versa. This notion of the veiled Muslim woman as 'rising above her designated position in a racialised visual order' echoes 'a familiar discourse of the immigrant Other exercising too much agency' (Patton, 2014, p. 196). Read against this context, we can see that masks temporarily overwrite the Western face, which probably partly explains the strength of emotion sparked off by mask mandates as well as the overwhelming focus of research on the effects that masking has on communication.

Power and Inequalities

As indicated above, it is necessary to set the micro-interactions that we have discussed so far in the broader context of power and inequalities. This is because masking practices are bound up with 'existing social divisions, fractures and inequalities' (Inglis & Almila, 2020, p. 253), as discussed in Chap. 2 in relation to feelings of dis/comfort in public spaces. Take age for example. The extent to which people entered public spaces varied by age (we are here excluding the significant virtual public realm that flourished during lockdowns when working from home, homeschooling, and socialising online became widespread). People over 70 were told to shield at the start of the pandemic in the UK and in other countries, while school pupils returned to classrooms before restrictions were lifted for adults. Research conducted during the height of the pandemic showed that many older people felt safer going into public spaces where pandemic measures, including masking, were adhered to and avoided spaces where masking was not prevalent (Brooks et al., 2022; Finlay et al., 2022).

How the public realm changed for people of working age was largely dependent on occupation. As noted above, compared to those working in privileged white-collar occupations, many of whom were able to work from home during the pandemic, those in lower-paid occupations were more likely to have to come into physical contact with customers and patients, thus exposing themselves to a higher risk of infection. This included hospital staff, public transport workers, supermarket cashiers, and delivery drivers, some of whom were on low pay and precarious contracts. Research has shown that the risk of infection and death from Covid-19 was highest for racialised minorities and those on low incomes, the two often intersecting in contemporary societies due to persistent racism (Clouston et al., 2021; Irizar et al., 2023).

Much of the research on the effects of masking on interactions during the pandemic did not take into consideration the ways in which mask wearing was a gendered and racialised experience that reflected existing inequalities. As discussed in Chap. 2, such inequalities shape the degree to which people can feel at ease in public spaces. Women and people from racialised minority groups were more likely to become the targets of verbal and physical aggression because of wearing a mask (Chang et al., 2021; Ren & Feagin, 2021). In the US and France, people of Asian origin reported that people more frequently avoided them in public or acted aggressively towards them (Kahn & Money, 2022; Wang et al., 2021). In the US, Black people reported that when they wore masks, they became the targets of increased surveillance by the public and the police alike (Inglis & Almila, 2020; Kahn & Money, 2022). Anderson (2015) has argued that in majority white countries such as the US, much of public space can be characterised as 'white space' where whiteness is the norm. The discomfort that racialised minorities feel in such white space was heightened during the pandemic, with mask wearing often acting as the catalyst for negative interactions.

What is at stake here is a person's ability to inhabit the public realm without undue attention being paid to them that would make them feel out of place (Ahmed, 2014). Horgan (2017) writes about the importance of mutual indifference as contributing to soft solidarity in urban contexts. This mutual indifference is based on minimal mutual recognition and allows each party to go about their business unaffected, and thus helps constitute strangerness as a social relation. Tonkiss (2003, p. 302, emphasis in original) calls this an ethics of indifference that bestows upon others the gift of privacy and the right 'to be left alone, *not* to be looked at'. This is something that people whose presence is deemed out of place—for example because of their skin colour, gender, or sexuality—and who are therefore noticed, cannot take for granted (Ahmed, 2014). As some of our observations attest, white and able-bodied persons such as us—who had previously enjoyed the privilege of anonymity and had access to the 'rights to and freedoms in the city' (Tonkiss, 2003, p. 298)—could during the pandemic find themselves in the unusual position of feeling "out of place" and even facing uncivil attention (Horgan, 2020) because of their choice to (not) wear a mask.

We contend that how the novelty of masking was dealt with in public interactions also speaks to wider issues of social control and power. During the pandemic, people's experiences of the public realm, and of how it changed, differed due to a mixture of pre-existing inequalities and newly emerging inequalities created by pandemic conditions. The adjustments in social relations brought on by masking reflected and brought into relief existing social divisions and inequalities. What for some was a hitherto unfamiliar experience of being noticed in public, is one that women and sexual and racialised minorities have routinely felt on their skin also pre-pandemic.

Conclusion

The height of the Covid-19 pandemic offered a natural "laboratory" where people were visibly and consciously working out the rules of interaction. This entailed both visible and measurable adjustments to frequency and length of interactions but also the more intangible dimension of how people experienced interactions in public in a situation where the rules of interaction were constantly and at times rapidly changing.

In such a setting, some fundamental features of interactional rules came to the fore, as did the fact that people are adept at negotiating them. The pandemic setting highlighted that interactional rules vary from space to space and depending on the type of relationship. Interactional rules are also ambiguous, especially at the threshold of the public and the private. Masking mandates and social distancing rules, because they unsettled taken-for-granted assumptions about public interactions, brought into relief the work that people are constantly having to do in order to figure out how to act in any given situation. This work became in many instances conscious as people moved across different types of space that required different masking practices. We have also shed light on the vital role that interactional discomfort plays in figuring out what the new rules of interaction are in a transformed public realm.

The sudden emergence of masking thus revealed something fundamental about the nature of the public realm, including the underlying power inequalities that underpin all social interactions and the role that trust and solidarity play in constituting "safe" stranger interactions (Horgan, 2017; Tonkiss, 2003). We argue that, therefore, all of the above questions concerning public interactions and how they are negotiated must always be explored with an understanding of the intersectional inequalities that underpin them. Our analysis of masking has also allowed us to draw attention to the cultural contingency of the notion of "face". This has revealed the emphasis on the visual within Eurocentric understandings of what allows for successful face-to-face interactions. This perhaps helps explain why masking in particular, in contrast to social distancing, gave rise to heightened emotional responses. These responses were, more often than not, couched in moral terms, as we go on to explore in Chap. 4.

References

Ahmed, S. (2014). *The cultural politics of emotion* (2nd ed.). Edinburgh University Press.

Anderson, E. (2015). The white space. *Sociology of Race and Ethnicity, 1*(1), 10–21.

Askarizad, R., Jinliao, H., & Jafari, S. (2021). The influence of COVID-19 on the societal mobility of urban spaces. *Cities, 119*, 103388.

Bhasin, T., Butcher, C., Gordon, E., Hallward, M., & LeFebvre, R. (2020). Does Karen wear a mask? The gendering of COVID-19 masking rhetoric. *International Journal of Sociology and Social Policy, 40*(9/10), 929–937.

Bogart, K. R. (2021). Masks in the time of COVID-19 as an inadvertent simulation of facial paralysis. *Disability & Society, 36*(5), 840–843.

Bourdieu, P. (1992). *The logic of practice*. Polity Press.

Brooks, E., Mohammadi, S., Mortenson, W. B., Backman, C. L., Tsukura, C., Rash, I., Chan, J., & Miller, W. C. (2022). 'Make the Most of the situation'. Older adults' experiences during COVID-19: A longitudinal, qualitative study. *Journal of Applied Gerontology, 41*(10), 2205–2213.

Calbi, M., Langiulli, N., Ferroni, F., Montalti, M., Kolesnikov, A., Gallese, V., & Umiltà, M. A. (2021). The consequences of COVID-19 on social interactions: An online study on face covering. *Scientific Reports, 11*(1), 2601.

Carbon, C.-C. (2020). Wearing face masks strongly confuses counterparts in Reading emotions. *Frontiers in Psychology, 11.*

Chang, H. J. (Julie), Min, S., Woo, H., & Yurchisin, J. (2021). Mask-wearing behavior during the COVID-19 pandemic: A cross-cultural comparison between the United States and South Korea. *Family and Consumer Sciences Research Journal, 50*(1), 5–26.

Chester, M. et al. (2023). The COVID-19 pandemic, mask-wearing, and emotion recognition during latechildhood. *Social Development, 32*(1), 315–328. https://doi.org/10.1111/sode.12631.

Clouston, S. A. P., Natale, G., & Link, B. G. (2021). Socioeconomic inequalities in the spread of coronavirus-19 in the United States: A examination of the emergence of social inequalities. *Social Science & Medicine, 268*, 113554. https://doi.org/10.1016/j.socscimed.2020.113554

Collins, R. (2020). Social distancing as a critical test of the micro-sociology of solidarity. *American Journal of Cultural Sociology, 8*(3), 477–497.

Crandall, C. S., Bahns, A. J., & Gillath, O. (2022). Do masks affect social interaction? *Journal of Applied Social Psychology, 52*(12), 1172–1178.

Culpeper, J. (1996). Towards an anatomy of impoliteness. *Journal of Pragmatics, 25*(3), 349–367.

Deleuze, G., & Guattari, F. (1987). *A thousand plateaus: Capitalism and schizophrenia.* Translated by Massumi, B. Minneapolis and. University of Minnesota Press.

Drury, J., & Stokoe, E. (2022). The interactional production and breach of new norms in the time of COVID-19: Achieving physical distancing in public spaces. *British Journal of Social Psychology, 61*(3), 971–990.

Finlay, J. M., Meltzer, G., Cannon, M., & Kobayashi, L. C. (2022). Aging in place during a pandemic: Neighborhood engagement and environments since the COVID-19 pandemic onset. *The Gerontologist, 62*(4), 504–518.

Frega, R. (2015). The normative structure of the ordinary. *European Journal of Pragmatism and American Philosophy, VII*(1), 1–22.

Garfinkel, H. (1967). *Studies in Ethnomethodology.* Wiley.

Goffman, E. (1963). *Behavior in public places: Notes on the social Organization of Gatherings.* Free Press.

Goffman, E. (1967). *Interaction ritual: Essays on face-to-face behavior.* Pantheon Books.

Goffman, E. (1971). *Relations in public: Microstudies of the public order.* Basic Books.

Grundmann, F., Epstude, K., & Scheibe, S. (2021). Face masks reduce emotion-recognition accuracy and perceived closeness. *PLoS One, 16*(4), e0249792.

Hanna, E., Martin, G., Campbell, A., Connolly, P., Fearon, K., & Markham, S. (2022). Experiences of face mask use during the COVID-19 pandemic: A qualitative study. *Sociology of Health & Illness, 44*(9), 1481–1499.

Harms, A. (2020). Fortifying breath in this moment of spray: Face masks beyond COVID-19. *Social Anthropology, 28*(2), 277–278.

Homans, N. C., & Vroegop, J. L. (2021). Impact of face masks in public spaces during COVID-19 pandemic on daily life communication of cochlear implant users. *Laryngoscope Investigative Otolaryngology, 6*(3), 531–539.

Horgan, M. (2017). Interaction, indifference, injustice: Elements of a normative theory of urban solidarity. In F. Kurasawa (Ed.), *Interrogating the social: A critical sociology for the 21st century* (pp. 61–93). Springer International Publishing.

Horgan, M. (2020). Urban interaction ritual: Strangership, civil inattention and everyday incivilities in public space. *Pragmatics, 30*(1), 116–141.

Inglis, D., & Almila, A.-M. (2020). Un-masking the mask: Developing the sociology of facial politics in pandemic times and after. *SocietàMutamentoPolitica, 11*(21), 251–257.

Iranmanesh, A., & Alpar Atun, R. (2021). Reading the changing dynamic of urban social distances during the COVID-19 pandemic via Twitter. *European Societies, 23*(supl), S872–S886. https://doi.org/10.1080/14616696.2020.1846066.

Irizar, P., Pan, D., Kapadia, D., Bécares, L., Sze, S., Taylor, H., Amele, S., Kibuchi, E., Divall, P., Gray, L. J., Nellums, L. B., Katikireddi, S. V., & Pareek, M. (2023). Ethnic inequalities in COVID-19 infection, hospitalisation, intensive care admission, and death: A global systematic review and meta-analysis of over 200 million study participants. *eClinicalMedicine*, 1, 101877–24. https://doi.org/10.1016/j.eclinm.2023

James, A. C. (2020). Don't stand so close to me: Public spaces, behavioral geography, and COVID-19. *Dialogues in Human Geography, 10*(2), 187–190.

Jasiński, A. (2020). Public space or safe space—Remarks during the COVID-19 pandemic. *Technical Transactions, 117*(1).

Joas, H. (1990). The creativity of action and the intersubjectivity of reason: Mead's pragmatism and social theory. *Transactions of the Charles S. Peirce Society, 26*(2), 165–194.

Kahn, K. B., & Money, E. E. L. (2022). (un)masking threat: Racial minorities experience race-based social identity threat wearing face masks during COVID-19. *Group Processes & Intergroup Relations, 25*(4), 871–891.

Katila, J., Gan, Y., & Goodwin, M. H. (2020). Interaction rituals and 'social distancing': New haptic trajectories and touching from a distance in the time of COVID-19. *Discourse Studies, 22*(4), 418–440.

Lo Iacono, S., Przepiorka, W., Buskens, V., Corten, R., & van de Rijt, A. (2021). Covid-19 vulnerability and perceived norm violations predict loss of social trust: A pre-post study. *Social Science & Medicine, 291*, 114513.

Long, E., Patterson, S., Maxwell, K., Blake, C., Bosó Pérez, R., Lewis, R., McCann, M., Riddell, J., Skivington, K., Wilson-Lowe, R., & Mitchell,

K. R. (2022). COVID-19 pandemic and its impact on social relationships and health. *Journal of Epidemiology and Community Health, 76*(2), 128.

Mehta, V. (2020). The new proxemics: COVID-19, social distancing, and sociable space. *Journal of Urban Design, 25*(6), 669–674.

Mheidly, N., Fares, M. Y., Zalzale, H., & Fares, J. (2020). Effect of face masks on interpersonal communication during the COVID-19 pandemic. *Frontiers in Public Health, 8.*

Moors, A. (2009). The Dutch and the face-veil: The politics of discomfort. *Social Anthropology, 17*(4), 393–408.

Patton, C. (2014). Defacing Levinas: Vision, veiling and the ethics of republican citizenship in France. *Social Identities, 20*(2–3), 186–198.

Perini, M., & Sciara, S. (2022). Wearing an anti-COVID face mask predisposes to spontaneity and ideas' expression in social interactions: Findings from a pilot experiment. *Trends in Psychology, 30*(4), 718–728.

Pfaller, L. (2020). Theorizing the virus: Abjection and the COVID-19 pandemic. *International Journal of Sociology and Social Policy, 40*(9/10), 821–829.

Ren, J., & Feagin, J. (2021). Face mask symbolism in anti-Asian hate crimes. *Ethnic and Racial Studies, 44*(5), 746–758.

Ruba, A. L., & Pollak, S. D. (2020). Children's emotion inferences from masked faces: Implications for social interactions during COVID-19. *PLoS One, 15*(12), e0243708.

Scambler, G. (2020). Covid-19 as a "breaching experiment": Exposing the fractured society. *Health Sociology Review, 29*(2), 140–148. https://doi.org/10.1080/14461242.2020.1784019.

Sikka, T. (2021). Feminist materialism and COVID-19: The agential activation of everyday objects. *NORA—Nordic Journal of Feminist and Gender Research, 29*(1), 4–16.

Tavory, I. (2018). Between situations: Anticipation, rhythms, and the theory of interaction. *Sociological Theory, 36*(2), 117–133.

Tavory, I., & Fine, G. (2020). Disruption and the theory of the interaction order. *Theory and Society, 49*(3), 365–385.

Tonkiss, F. (2003). The ethics of indifference: Community and solitude in the city. *International Journal of Cultural Studies, 6*(3), 297–311.

Van Gorp, B. (2021). Face masks as floating signifiers during the COVID-19 pandemic in Belgium. *Visual Studies, 36*(2), 124–132.

Wang, S., Chen, X., Li, Y., Luu, C., Yan, R., & Madrisotti, F. (2021). 'I'm more afraid of racism than of the virus!': Racism awareness and resistance among Chinese migrants and their descendants in France during the COVID-19 pandemic. *European Societies, 23*(sup1), S721–S742.

Zetterberg, L., Santosa, A., Ng, N., Karlsson, M., & Eriksson, M. (2021). *Impact of COVID-19 on Neighborhood social support and social interactions in Umeå municipality* (p. 3). Frontiers in Sustainable Cities.

CHAPTER 4

Masks, Lay Moralities, and Moral Practice

Abstract This chapter explores how new moral practices and lay moralities developed in relation to masking during the height of the Covid-19 pandemic. We argue that the moral significance of masking led to lay moralities around masking being constructed and enacted in ways that were of deep significance to people during the pandemic, but which are mostly overlooked in dominant social scientific interpretations of masking. Likewise, these positions look past how interactionally moulded orders of moral practice around masking developed, which engendered emergent modes of enacting, appraising, and contesting "proper" masking conduct. A key argument for this chapter is that masking during the pandemic should be considered as an interactional moral phenomena, that developed in relation to unfolding knowledge that moulded new norms of practice, and within which people assumed moral positions and responsibilities in ways they had to figure out in relation to the visible materiality of the mask as a particularly interactional moral thing. Finally, the chapter discusses the moral contestation that developed around masking, arguing that such contestation also requires a greater consideration of interaction and social discourse than is given in current explanations.

Keywords Masks • Lay morality • Moral practice • Interaction • Materiality • Moral foundations theory

O. Abbott et al., *Masking in the Pandemic*, Consumption and Public Life, https://doi.org/10.1007/978-3-031-45781-4_4

Introduction

The profound moral significance of the Covid-19 pandemic has not been lost on academic commentators of all stripes, including sociologists, philosophers, psychologists, health professionals, and political scientists (Bos et al., 2020; Graham et al., 2020; Lupton et al., 2021; Vinay et al., 2021; Altman, 2022; Tarry et al., 2022). The severe (but unevenly distributed) health risks and novel social restrictions brought each of us face to face with the kind of moral questions that are ordinarily reserved for philosophy seminars. The pandemic engendered a raft of new and complicated moral decision-making at all levels of significance: from the 'grim calculus' weighed by politicians (The Economist, 2020) and the traumatising triaging undertaken by medical staff (Vinay et al., 2021), to decisions of what each of us needed to do to protect our own vulnerable kin (Cornelius et al., 2021) and what became more "everyday" decisions about how to make lockdown life 'livable': how to ensure our children are schooled, our lonely contacted, and our interactions made safe (Mollborn et al., 2021; Twamley et al., 2022, p. 85). As well as the complex novel moral decisions faced by all of us, people regularly assumed responsibilities, reached out to others, and sought to do their bit (Sitrin and Colectiva Sembrar, 2020; Carlsen et al., 2021). Indeed, amongst the devastation, suffering, hoarding, and regular exhibitions of selfishness and obstinance, the well-documented morally concerned and concerted action of ordinary people is easily forgotten (Sitrin and Colectiva Sembrar, 2020; Carlsen et al., 2021; Hellmann et al., 2021; Muqsith et al., 2021; Sin et al., 2021; Wider et al., 2022).

At an everyday level, face masks became an object through which a great deal of moral meaning and moral work was channelled. In a short space of time, face masks went from being an unusual and perhaps negatively regarded practice in the UK (given the moral significance of faces in the West, discussed in Chap. 3), to being touted as a potential tool for personal protection, to being discouraged on the grounds of moral necessity for non-health workers to not use up depleted stocks of PPE (Personal Protective Equipment), to being stipulated by the medical community as a public health imperative that allows us to protect others (Cheng et al., 2020). Subsequently, masking became a 'symbol of care', an object of moral judgement, and an emblem of political-moral contestation (Lupton et al., 2021, p. xiii). For a short period in the UK and elsewhere, masking came to be seen as the "right thing to do" by many in the face of the pandemic, with studies identifying the protection of others as the most significant motivation for people wearing masks in public (Rieger, 2020; Martinelli et al., 2021; Warnock-Parkes et al., 2021). As noted in the previous chapter, masking consequently became a tangible social practice around which new orders of moral interaction emerged. The materiality of masks meant they became simultaneously a medium of protection, 'techno-moral mediators' (Ji, 2020, p. 1) that facilitated moral decisions and allowed interactions to be had and appraised, and a means for showing moral concern, for representing oneself as a responsible person, and for signalling one's (contested) moral stance towards the pandemic and its associated restrictions (Graham et al., 2020; Kim & Chung, 2021; Lupton et al., 2021).

Masking during the Covid-19 pandemic (especially in Westernised countries in which wearing a face mask in public for health reasons was virtually non-existent) provides sociologists with a unique opportunity to observe the development of a moral norm, practice, and form of lay normativity "before our eyes", as it were. However, many of the dominant accounts given of masking and other Covid-related measures are not adept at exploring the moral experience of masking at an everyday level, nor how interactional moral norms around masking developed. Firstly in academic opinion pieces and then in peer-reviewed literature, sociological accounts have drawn most heavily on Foucault's concepts of disciplinarity and biopolitics to analyse Covid-related rules, with good reason (Hannah et al., 2020; O'Farrell, 2020; Sotiris, 2020; Sylvia, 2020; Wu, 2020). In the social sciences more broadly, moral attitudes towards Covid-19 measures have mostly been considered through applications of "moral foundations theory" (Graham et al., 2020; Chan, 2021; Tarry et al., 2022; Zhou et al., 2022). Moral foundations theory (MFT) argues our moral attitudes towards social phenomena (such as political messages, facemasks, and vaccines) are pre-orientated by moral foundations wired in our brains through our childhood moral development (Haidt, 2013). While of great relevance to describing aspects of social existence during the pandemic, Foucauldian and MFT perspectives alike elide the lay moralities and the interactional moral orders that developed around masking. The first part of this chapter looks at how lay moralities developed in relation to shifting scientific and political discourse. Building on Chap. 3, the second section considers how these discourses and lay moralities were translated into interactional practices, yielding new facets of an emergent moral order around masking, within which lay moralities were constructed and negotiated, and behaviours judged and contested. The final section applies these discussions to moral contestation around masking, arguing that theories of moral foundations can only take us so far in explaining moral contestation at an everyday level.

Masking and Moral Concern

In this section, we consider how the proliferation of masking in response to the Covid-19 pandemic engendered the development of lay moralities about masking. We illuminate how moral perspectives and senses of responsibility were assumed at an everyday level in ways that are often elided in dominant social scientific framings of the pandemic. Yet, masking also tells us something about the character of lay moralities in social life and their role in the everyday sense-making undertaken by everyone in the face of the pandemic.

The resurgence of sociological accounts of morality in recent decades has coincided with, and in many important respects developed in relation to, greater emphasis on everyday life perspectives in sociology (Abbott, 2020; Gilman, 2022). As a result, significant focus has been dedicated to "lay moralities" across a range of topics (e.g. personal relationships (Burr, 2009), consumption (Grauel, 2016), medical interactions (Heritage & Lindstrom, 1998), class-based judgements of taste (Sayer, 2011)). Lay moralities, also referred to as everyday or mundane moralities, are comprised of an amalgam of people's ordinary moral evaluations, interpretations of what is right and wrong, senses of responsibility and care, as well as routine moralised judgements, appraisals, and attributions of culpabilities taken towards others and ourselves (Keane, 2010; Ekberg et al., 2021). Rather than being rare or extraordinary, such lay moralities are part and parcel of people's ordinary sense-making of the social world of which they are part (DeNora, 2014). The ordinariness of lay moralities reflects the fact that we are beings who are both vulnerable and reflexive, and whose development from childhood occurs to a significant degree through normative integration and evaluative judgement within the social relationships upon which we depend (Benhabib, 1992; May, 2013). Our moral socialisation within an entanglement of direct and extended social relationships means our lay moralities reflect shared social meanings and social forces, while taking shape from our specific experiences, dispositions, circumstances, and relationships.

The recontextualisation of the moral into the everyday lives of ordinary actors has been key to bringing morality into the domain of sociological consideration once again. Yet, the tendency to straightforwardly cast people's normative evaluations in terms of conventions and institutional imposition remains common in the social sciences. While of great relevance to describing social life, taken alone such approaches tend to miscast 'people's first person evaluative relation to the world' and undervalues the significance that normative questions about 'what is good or bad about what is happening [...] and of how to act, and what to do for the best' have to people's everyday lives (Sayer, 2011, pp. 1–2).

In the UK and in other countries in which masking was previously very rare, clearly the practice of masking proliferated so rapidly as a new norm because it became legally stipulated. The introductory chapter charts how masking rates in the UK rose steeply when masking mandates were first introduced (on 24 July 2020) and fell fairly rapidly after the second masking mandate (reintroduced between 30 November 2021 and 26 January 2022) was lifted. It should be noted that rates of people who said they had worn a face mask in a public place in the last 7 days remained around the 60% mark between the time that the UK's mask mandate was first removed on 19 July 2021 and the reintroduction of the masking mandate in November 2021, and indeed most continued to support the reintroductions of masking rules after the masking mandate was first lifted (Office for National Statistics, 2021; YouGov, 2021). Nevertheless, these statistics generally indicate how masking behaviours in the UK have closely followed national mandates (whilst not being determined by them).

This says interesting things about the following of rules and about how populations can be mobilised. Applications of Foucault's concepts of disciplinarity and biopolitics to Covid-related rules have thus dominated sociological accounts of masking (Hannah et al., 2020; O'Farrell, 2020; Sylvia, 2020; Sotiris, 2020; Wu, 2020). Considering Foucault developed his concept of disciplinarity in the context of governing plague towns in Europe, and considering his concept of biopolitics refers specifically to the management of populations through the measurement and administration of health (Foucault, 2020), the pandemic seems tailor-made for academic analysis of Covid-related behaviours through these concepts. Yet while appropriately applied to studying how lockdowns and other Covid-related measures were imposed, these perspectives mostly overlook something important about how people experienced their responses to the pandemic and its associated behaviours.

Indeed, such perspectives tell us considerably less about how people made sense of and enacted their own senses of responsibility (and contestation) through the enactment of behaviours like masking, often even when these were not mandated. As noted in previous discussions of how masking knowledge developed with a considerable degree of uncertainty, it is clear that the novel and rapidly emerging nature of the pandemic regularly yielded the kind of opacity from which moral sense-making springs (Morgan, 2014). Mask wearing was actively discouraged by UK policymakers at the start of the pandemic, both on the grounds that evidence of their utility was mixed and due to concerns that members of the public would "use up" stocks of PPE which were then in short supply in the NHS (National Health Service) and care homes (The Royal Society, 2020). Within the swirl of mixed and unfolding scientific and political discourse, at least in the UK, calls for masking mandates to be introduced did not flow in one direction, from government to populace. As well as proliferating as a practice prior to government rules, the introduction of masking mandates lagged behind public support for the measure, and mandates were removed in opposition to prevailing public opinion (Banerjee et al., 2021; YouGov, 2021).

Even in the messy context of the UK, for many, seemingly most, masking became part of what they took to be the right and responsible thing to do, coming to symbolise care and concern for others within the threat posed by the pandemic. Amongst emerging scientific discourse and institutional guidance, for more people than not, masks came to be indicative of performance of social expectation in a Goffmanian sense, but also in the deeper sense of presenting oneself as being morally sound, and as exhibiting care and concern for others, signalling to others that we are willing to do our part in curbing the "R-number"[1] and protecting the vulnerable. Yet masking became much more than a medium of moral performance, significant as this is. The importance of masking to the protection of others meant it became for many an object of responsibility, a practice that they *should* do not just because it is socially emblematic or legally mandated, but rather because it is what they felt was the right thing to do in response to the deadliness of the virus.

[1] 'The reproduction number (R) is the average number of secondary infections produced by a single infected person[…] If R is greater than 1, the [pandemic] is growing, if R is less than 1 the [pandemic] is shrinking' (GOV.UK, 2022). The R-number thus became a central figure to understandings of how the pandemic was developing.

Indeed, studies of attitudes towards the adoption of masking and other Covid-19 restrictions found motivations for masking were not driven simply by legal mandates (which were easily ignored, often with little consequence), but also because, for many people, such behaviours came to be tied to senses of moral responsibility (Kim & Chung, 2021; Martinelli et al., 2021; Mollborn et al., 2021; Oosterhoff et al., 2020; Rieger, 2020; Warnock-Parkes et al., 2021). Notably, a number of studies indicated that while self-protection weighed heavily in people's attitudes towards mask wearing, the most significant reason people gave for wearing a mask in public was the protection of others (Oosterhoff et al., 2020; Rieger, 2020; Martinelli et al., 2021; Warnock-Parkes et al., 2021). This was found to be particularly significant as a motivation for younger people, generally the lowest risk group, for engaging with Covid-19 measures (Oosterhoff et al., 2020). Whilst we should be critical of any simple interpretation of reported motives as evidence of people's inner psychological drives (Mills, 1940), as The Royal Society (2020) noted, such findings do suggest that messaging based on the altruism of masking were widely accepted by UK publics and were seen as integral to ensuring high uptake of the practice.

Masking thus became a 'symbol of care' and responsibility, a particularly tangible act through which concern for others and for the pandemic could be made manifest (Lupton et al., 2021, p. xiii). In their analysis of moral evaluations of Covid-19 behaviours in Korea, Kim and Chung (2021, p. 4) note that although masking was already a common practice prior to Covid-19 in Korea due to concerns about pollution, a distinction emerged among Koreans in which a 'mask used to protect against fine dust pollution is for personal safety, while a mask used in the COVID-19 outbreak is an act of social responsibility for others'. While masking for the protection of one's own health is a moral practice focused on individuals' bodies, Covid-19 imbued masking with meanings of social responsibility and the protection of others that gave the practice a new moral significance.

Part of the issue with some of the more simplistically applied Foucauldian perspectives is that they 'downplay [mask] wearers' moral agency by reducing them to obedient subjects' (Ji, 2020, p. 3). As Sayer (2011, p. 2 italics original) reminds us, integral sociological concerns with institutional power, inequality, and social division means it is easy to lose sight of how, at an everyday level, 'we are *beings whose relation to the world is one of concern*', who are frequently preoccupied with normative evaluations of what we should do for the best, what we think is right, how people act and how they should act in relation to others, and more general questions of how things are and how they should be. This proved to be the case with masking as a response to Covid-19.

Across the globe, masking (and also not masking, as discussed below) became part of people's lay moralities. Yet Foucauldian perspectives commonly used to provide a sociological perspective on Covid-19 behaviours often reduce the force and flow of everyday moral experience. They tend to elide the social significance of lay normativity and moral sense-making undertaken by ordinary people in relation to shifting scientific and social discourses, within which masking became translated into an object of moral practice, concern, and contestation. Such perspectives are also not adept at recognising how new moral orders surrounding masking were formed through interactions, which then produced the contours of moral practice, judgment, and contestation in relation to facemasks. A key argument of what follows, then, is that masking during the pandemic should be considered as an interactional moral phenomena that developed as unfolding knowledges moulded new norms of practice, within which people assumed moral positions and responsibilities in ways they had to figure out in relation to the visible materiality of the mask as a particularly interactional moral thing.

Masks and Moral Practice

Masking was just one aspect of lay moralities that developed during the pandemic. Yet, the visible materiality of masks, with their protective and medicalised qualities (discussed in Chap. 2), meant masking assumed a particularly salient role as a tangible practice that people could *do* and be seen to do: masks allowed people to feel they were doing their bit to ameliorate the pandemic, and became an object through which moral attitudes towards the pandemic could be channelled. Masking thus became for many a moral practice. And as a tangible moral practice, interactional norms of correct performance and modes of judging, correcting, and accounting quickly developed around masking through the interactions that masks facilitated or hindered. As noted in Chap. 3, Scambler (2020) argues that the devastation Covid-19 wrought means the pandemic acted as something of an unbounded "breaching experiment". As will be argued in this section, with ordinary interactional orders suddenly suspended, and as a key component of pandemic interactions, masking practices developed their own interactional moral order norms, which extended beyond that provided by institutional guidance.

In dramatic fashion, the pandemic and its associated restrictions shattered the accepted moral order of ordinary social conduct in ways that might have seemed unimaginable beforehand (Ekberg et al., 2021). Many previously acceptable practices (such as interactions with families and friends, the use of public services, and physical greetings) were rendered unacceptable and illegal, while many novel behaviours (such as masking and social distancing) became part of the social expectation of interactions. In a short space of time, 'adherence to pandemic rules became morally expected, and moral concerns about actual or potential violations to these rules became relevant in and through social interaction during this period' (Ekberg et al., 2021, p. 666). From an interactionist perspective, the rapid shifts in expected behaviour engendered by the pandemic provides almost unparalleled insight into 'how accountable actions and a moral order are negotiated in and through our social interactions when our taken-for-granted "natural facts of life" change' (Ekberg et al., 2021, p. 666).

The interactional moral order that developed around face masks is fundamentally tied to their materiality. Masks became not just a medical thing that protected from the virus, but also a *moral* thing (Balmer et al., 2021). The visibility of face masks meant they played an integral role in affording moral decision-making, in allowing situations and people to be judged and appraised, in facilitating the assumption of care towards others, and in exhibiting oneself as a morally responsible and knowledgeable actor within the complexities and dangers of the pandemic (Ji, 2020; Kim & Chung, 2021; Lupton et al., 2021). Drawing on Verbeek (2008), Ji (2020, p. 1) discusses face masks as 'techno-moral mediators', in which objects assume moral status and constitute significant aspects of human moral agency. Masks mediate between wearers, non-wearers, and the environment of which they are part, making 'people aware of a set of morally relevant distinctions and [...] shap[ing] the parameters for human practice and experience in the epidemic [*sic*]' (Ji, 2020, p. 1).

Masks afforded the capacity to adhere with legal stipulations of how to act (e.g. technically only being allowed in a shop if wearing a face covering). Yet, the role of masking as a visible mediator of appropriate moral conduct in the new rules of the social world illuminates how 'pandemic culture and accompanying moral order was produced within and through social interaction' (Ekberg et al., 2021, p. 666). As Ekberg et al.'s (2021, p. 669) conversation analysis of interactions between patients and medical staff during the pandemic shows, actions that were previously 'morally non-accountable', such as seeing friends or not wearing a mask, suddenly required justification, explanation, and reaffirmation of one's awareness of the rules within interactional exchanges. Within these interactions, moral orders were reproduced and negotiated in several ways. Firstly, through people attempting to enact correct action within these new rules and parameters. Secondly, through the judgement and condemnation of the action of others. And thirdly, through people accounting for, apologising for, or seeking to correct their own action when potential violations occur (Ekberg et al., 2021). The same is true of how moral orders surrounding face masks were constructed and reconstructed through interactions.

On the first point, masking became a visible medium for correct moral performance (Ji, 2020; Kim & Chung, 2021). Masking practices entailed not just proper adherence to legally stipulated rules of when to mask, but also came to frame the contours of appropriate and morally sound action. In situations where rules were clear such as in shops and on public transport, failure to don a mask could result in denial of entry, although the strictness of this enforcement was limited or readily excused. Yet (as alluded to in the observations given in Chap. 3), there developed among many an impelling urge to display awareness of proper conduct, even in situations where the rules were unclear, for example as masks were hurriedly fumbled when passing someone outside with whom we would like to converse, or as we encountered someone at a distance in our otherwise deserted office building.

Secondly, in addition to (or perhaps more so than) formalised rules, this new norm quickly became normatively monitored in interaction through emergent behaviours that became familiar. Criticising looks, shared expressions of exasperation, and pointedly giving a wide berth to those unmasked became commonplace means for passing judgement and contrasting correct with incorrect performance of the moral order. Interactional practices of appraisal (such as smiling, glaring, avoidance, prejudicial terms such as "covidiot" and "half-mast masked") sprung up as mask-wearers 'socially "reward[ed]" each other but "punish[ed]" others who do not wear a mask' (Betsch et al., 2020, p. 21851). Such judgement took flight in public settings, in condemnatory conversations with friends, and in the comments of social media (e.g. as people lambasted those who refused to wear masks in shops or on a plane, or who failed to mask despite being aware they had been in contact with someone with Covid-19) (Betsch et al., 2020; Kim & Chung, 2021). Elsewhere, with an additional moral force accrued by their status as emblems of the fight against the pandemic, some medical staff took to social media to illuminate the moral significance of following (or not following) Covid-19 restrictions (Lydall, 2021; Glasdam et al., 2022). In a particularly telling example for the present topic, medical staff used social media platforms to share pictures of their faces rubbed raw from hours of wearing medical masks on Covid-19 wards, with a view to putting the small moral sacrifice of members of the public wearing a mask for a short while into context (CBS News, 2020; Glasdam et al., 2022).

Thirdly, as with Ekberg et al.'s (2021) study, for many (including for the authors of this book) there thus developed a felt need for non-compliant masking behaviours to be explained or corrected: apologising, stressing profusely that we are never one to forget our mask, pulling a collar over the mouth and nose, or awkwardly attempting to hold a broken mask to one's face. Accounting and judgement also intersected for those exempt from masking due to disabilities, who regularly felt the need to find ways to make hidden disabilities visible to allay everything from questioning looks to aggressive verbal attacks (Ferguson, 2020; Hanna et al., 2022). Such practices exemplify the continual 'correcting, sanctioning, criticizing [and] approving' of others in interaction that Goffman argued is an ordinary feature of how interactional orders are maintained and adjusted (Frega, 2015). Yet interactions within the pandemic in relation to masking illuminate the emergent processes and practices that arise as part of the establishment, maintenance, and negotiation of the moral order within a newly engendered interactional circumstance.

Through actions we all became familiar with for a brief period, people 'displayed concern for showing others that they were aware of what was or was not acceptable behaviour during the pandemic', thus affirming, negotiating, and situating oneself in relation to the new moral order in their interactions (Ekberg et al., 2021, p. 669). Just as in classic ethnomethodological accounts of how moral orders are sustained and rectified in practice, through interactions people sought to display their moral rectitude, their knowledge of the moral order, and their disdain for those who had breached normative parameters. Yet the enactment of a moral order is never simply a case of straightforwardly enacting rules, even when legally prescribed (Heritage & Lindstrom, 1998). The vicissitudes of contextual circumstance and intersubjective interaction mean indeterminacy, "messiness", and interpretation are endemic to social encounters (Emirbayer & Maynard, 2010). This is especially true of interactions during the pandemic, where a new moral order emerged, changed, and rescinded rapidly in relation to often ambiguous guidance.

In the UK, even when regulations were at their strictest, there remained an opacity in stipulations that needed to be judged and negotiated, often *in situ*. The necessity of masking outside remained unclear and situationally variable, producing moments of uncertainty, such as cautious discussion amongst socially distanced groups of friends about whether masks need to be kept on for outside liaisons. Other spaces, such as outside the school gate busy with other parents, were also less than clear in terms of what was stipulated and what was the right thing to do, with varying interpretations and levels of diligence adding further layers of opacity. As Sophie noted,

> *Sophie (January, 2021): In September 2020 when schools reopened, there was no mandate for wearing masks when dropping off or picking up (despite the mass of parents there), and whilst I knew and was clear on my moral position that wearing a mask is the right thing to do, there were very few people wearing them, and as such the certainty lessens and one starts to feel self-conscious and foolish trying to have a conversation with someone who is unmasked. In contrast, going to a supermarket when masking is mandated and seeing everyone in them, an observation of someone unmasked and standing next to another unmasked person may lead to a moral judgement that they "should" be wearing a mask. We come to feel secure and more certain in our masking practices.*

Other situations of rules produced indeterminacy through their farcical nature. For example, there was a period in the UK where pubs and restaurants were open but it was necessary to wear a mask until seated at one's table. Once seated, people could freely remove their masks regardless of their proximity to others, thus leading to masking while standing up feeling like something of a charade (Hanna et al., 2022). While masks set parameters for actions and judgements, they also often became mediums of moral uncertainty in situations where it was not clear if masking was necessary or if we would be judged for not masking.

Significantly, as with other moral practices, situational and intersubjective influences proved to be more decisive than formalised rules on when and where people felt it necessary to mask (Rieger, 2020; Dillard et al., 2021). Early into the pandemic, commentators illuminated the significance of interactional and contextual influences becoming relevant to mask wearing, and how greater concentrations of mask wearing is likely to produce greater uptake of the behaviour (Rieger, 2020; Woodcock & Schultz, 2021). This proved to be particularly significant in people's decisions to wear a mask in a busy outdoor setting or in a group of associates meeting outside (Woodcock & Schultz, 2021). Furthermore, as Dillard et al. (2021, p. 1) note, practices of masking were 'diminished by the frequency with which respondents observed others not wearing a mask [...] and the frequency with which respondents observed others expressing disdain for masking'.

Masking allows us to witness the development, enactment, and maintenance of an emergent moral practice. But attitudes towards masks also reflect divergence. Between strongly politicised stances of pro- and anti-masking, attitudes diverged on varying levels of care, diligence, acquiescence, and reluctance. Rules rarely map straightforwardly on to practice, and with masks people applied, negated, challenged, adapted, forgot, got swept along with situations, and acted in response to the particulars of social context, leading to occasions of non- or partial compliance with masking expectations even among those mostly committed to masking (Rieger, 2020). This reflects the fact that masking practices, as with moral practices in general (Abbott, 2020), occur within multiple practical, normative, and intersubjective contexts and commitments. As discussed in Chap. 2, the materiality of masks meant they could easily be forgotten and regularly became uncomfortable (fogging up glasses, becoming stifling in hot weather, making us sweat, making our noses run, and sometimes making interaction hard). Such were the practicalities of masking that even clearly expressed moral positions towards masking did not necessarily translate straightforwardly into "correct" action in all social contexts. Indeed, as Sophie (January, 2021) observed, 'even a certain moral position such as that mask should be worn in all public places gives way to discomfort when faced with a non-masker who we may feel unable to say anything to', for example when faced with a friend, family member, or a boss whose attitudes to masking were somewhat more blasé (see also Rogers et al., 2020). And as Lupton et al. (2021) discuss, as masking rates began to decline, suddenly the feeling of correct, socially approved moral comportment often came to be replaced by wondering if people's sideways glances or raised eyebrows now meant they assumed us to be paranoid for continuing to wear a mask in a public setting. These points illuminate the complex intersubjective contexts and multiple normative commitments (such as feeling unable to challenge behaviours from certain people, or moralised expectations to appear friendly or to legitimise unmasked others) that moulded masking practices in practice.

Analysing practices of mask wearing moves us beyond the institutional imposition of masking mandates, allowing us to explore how broadly framed rules and moral attitudes about masking translated into the *in situ* establishment of a briefly assembled moral order of interaction. But considering masking in terms of moral practice, rather than in terms of institutionally prescribed compliance or "correct" moral judgement, also allows us to register the significance of "doing" morality in the context of ever-changing intersubjectively and practically situated social circumstance.

Masking, Moral Divisions, and Moral Foundations

Despite becoming for a short while part of the newly negotiated moral order of interactions, wearing a face mask in public or feeling that it is the right thing to do (as with other Covid-related restrictions) was by no means uniformly adopted. Indeed, this new moral order and its vernacular of judgement and appraisal were constituted through the designation of, and distinction from, those who were cast as selfish and irresponsible (Ekberg et al., 2021; Ji, 2020; Kim & Chung, 2021). These moralised interactions and judgements consequently provided fertile ground for designations of oppositions between maskers and non-maskers (Graham et al., 2020; Ji, 2020). A final point to be made, then, is that while social and scientific discourses led to masking becoming what many people took to be the proper thing to do, masking also became something of a fault line, a marker for "us" and "them" (Southerton, 2003). As Vanessa noted,

> Vanessa (January, 2021): *Masks might be a way of finding some kind of solid ground: at least we can easily identify who is "one of us". And when we spot "one of them"—either a fool who has fallen for the propaganda and is dutifully sporting a mask, or the "Covidiot" who refuses to listen to science and is defiantly spreading their germs to others—we feel justified in our judgment of them, whether silently endured or aggressively expressed.*

As several have noted, divisions in attitudes towards Covid-19 restrictions often seemed to align with more general political and moral divisions in Westernised societies. This has led to a body of literature applying Jonathon Haidt's "moral foundations theory" to explain differences in attitudes towards pandemic behaviours, including masking (Graham et al.,

2020; Qian & Yahara, 2020; Chan, 2021; Díaz & Cova, 2021; Heine & Wolters, 2021; Vartanova et al., 2021; Bruchmann & LaPierre, 2022; Nan et al., 2022; Tarry et al., 2022; Wang, 2022; Zhou et al., 2022). Indeed, moral foundations theory seems to be the most extensively applied explanation of Covid-related moral attitudes and behaviours, providing something of an accepted wisdom in the pages of many of the world's leading scientific journals.

Haidt's (2013) moral foundations theory (MFT) has been widely adopted in moral psychology, often as a tool for testing and explaining differences in moral attitudes that pertain to "culture war" type debates. The theory is firstly based on the argument that 'people in all cultures are born with the capacity to cultivate virtues based on all five foundations' that underpin moral cultures and intuitions (Haidt & Graham, 2009, p. 381). These foundations are (1) harm/care; (2) fairness/reciprocity; (3) ingroup/loyalty; (4) authority/respect; (5) purity/sanctity. Each of these foundations, according to Haidt, reflect evolutionary adaptions that have proved to be beneficial to the survival of the human species, which explains why cultural virtues based on these foundations have been shown to be cultivated in cultures across the world. Evolutionary in their basis, these moral foundations are 'prewired' in our brains from birth (Haidt, 2013, p. 153). They provide the foundations of moral learning, but the moral learning itself is not in-built. Instead, certain moral foundations come to be accented in our moral socialisation during childhood, thus reflecting the context and experiences of that socialisation.

These moral foundations are used to explain the well-tested argument that moral judgements are predominantly made intuitively, with moral reasoning mostly being constructed afterwards to justify our intuitive-led judgement (Haidt, 2013). The argument goes that our prewired moral foundations facilitate the making of moral judgements in a fraction of a second (Haidt, 2001; Ignatow, 2009). However, because moral reasoning is reflexive, people (and academic accounts) tend to assume their moral judgements, aversions, or preferences are guided by this reasoning. This, Haidt argues, is backwards: 'Moral intuitions arise automatically and almost instantaneously, long before moral reasoning has a chance to get started, and those first intuitions tend to drive our later reasoning', with people's moral reasoning being 'mostly post hoc constructions made up on the fly' (Haidt, 2013, pp. xx–xxi).

The third significant point from MFT is that people of different political-moral persuasions tend to be opposed because they have had different moral foundations accentuated in their upbringing. Not without some contestation (e.g. Blum, 2013; Harper & Rhodes, 2021), Haidt (2013) divides people into liberal and conservatives. This does not necessarily refer to partisan divides, but more refers to people with more liberal and conservative mindsets. MFT claims liberals accentuate just the first two of the five moral foundations: *avoiding harm/acting with care* and *acting with fairness/reciprocity*. These are labelled as "individualizing" foundations (Bruchmann & LaPierre, 2022; Tarry et al., 2022). Conservatives, on the other hand, are more likely to exhibit all five moral foundations, including a stronger emphasis on the last three foundations: *respecting authority*, *loyalty to ingroup*, and *concern for sanctity/purity*. These three foundations are referred to as "binding", and often entail a greater deference to tradition, something which those of liberal mindsets are less likely to accent (Graham et al., 2020; Chan, 2021; Wang, 2022). These differences in the accentuation of moral foundations, according to the theory, produce dispositional differences in how moral judgements are made. This point has been well-tested, with numerous studies indicating firstly that more liberally and conservatively minded people do indeed tend to accentuate these differences in moral disposition (whether or not these reflect or need to be referred to as neurologically wired foundations is a different matter), and secondly that these different emphases tend to pertain to respective support for or aversion towards political and moral issues about which liberals and conservatives tend to be divided (see Kivikangas et al. (2021) for review).

The application of MFT to masking and other Covid-related behaviours thus hypothesise and to some extent affirm that attitudes towards such practices are moulded by one's moral foundations. Indeed, soon into the pandemic a number of studies had identified correlations between non-compliance with Covid-19-related restrictions (including masking) and conservative moral foundations (Graham et al., 2020; Chan, 2021). Yet the precedence given to the assumed explanatory power of the MFT model means that much around political-moral dispositions is miscast or relegated in significance. For example, age and gender have been shown to be the most significant factors in the likelihood of Covid-19 measures (including masking) being followed (Haischer et al., 2020; Kim & Crimmins, 2020; Pasion et al., 2020; Twamley et al., 2022). Both these factors indicate something significant beyond political dispositions, such as gendered perceptions of risks and responsibilities, performances of masculinity, differing social pressures, and experiences of risk across the life course. Indeed, the significance of age is recognised in some of the applications of MFT to Covid-19 restrictions. Chan's (2021) study found notable age differences in how younger and older people associated loyalty and sanctity with wearing a facemask and staying at home. It is explained that some evidence suggests 'age predicts which moral foundations are stressed—with loyalty and sanctity more relevant for older than younger age groups' (Chan, 2021, p. 2). On a more theoretical point, that moral foundations shift with age would perhaps suggest that foundations are less neurally wired than is often implied. On a more specific point, it seems on a practical level that those at highest risk would be more inclined to take up protective Covid-19 measures (Kim & Crimmins, 2020) regardless of their political-moral dispositions.

The framing of MFT around foundations that guide a person's moral intuitions and thus inform a person's ideology leads to many applications implying some sort of natural affinity between political mindset and attitudes towards novel Covid-related restrictions. Yet this confluence seems to be not so straightforward (Ekici et al., 2021). A reasonably common critique of MFT is that the theory and the MFT questionnaire designed for applications of the theory reflects anglophone histories and experiences of conservativism, in which a reverence for tradition and patriotism is amalgamated with the freedom of the sovereign individual (Voelkel & Brandt, 2019; Harper & Rhodes, 2021; Kivikangas et al., 2021). As such, non-masking attitudes (which on the face of it seem to be quite contrary to the notion of "binding" moral foundations) could be found to be associated with conservative moral foundations in anglophone contexts. Yet, as several applications in other contexts such as France, Germany, and China found, in contrast to US-based studies, higher scores on "conservative" "binding" moral foundations were associated with higher levels of concern about Covid-19, higher uptake of preventative measures, and higher willingness for vaccines to be shared globally than liberal counterparts (Díaz & Cova, 2021; Ekici et al., 2021; Bruchmann & LaPierre, 2022; Wang, 2022).

Dillard et al. (2021, p. 9) remind us that 'the liberal-conservative continuum is a sloppy amalgamation of many underlying beliefs and values that happen to cohere at a given moment in history'. And these values and underlying beliefs happen to cohere not simply because of an alignment of moral dispositions (as significant as these may be), but also because of pervasive social discourse. Certainly, in more straightforward applications of the MFT model, the role of social influence and discourse in moulding masking attitudes is mostly unconsidered. Yet as we have seen, attitudes and behaviours changed regularly in relation to unfolding scientific and political discourse, in relation to perceived risks, and as rules were perceived as becoming incongruous (Kim & Crimmins, 2020; The Royal Society, 2020). As well as contested scientific and public messaging, masking also became intensely and intentionally weaponised by political actors for their own ends (Sahin & Ianosev, 2021). Social discourse is considered in Graham et al.'s (2020) more sophisticated application of the relationship between MFT, faith in Donald Trump, and defiance of Covid-19 restrictions. Yet, although the paper gives significant space to outlining the anti-masking rhetoric espoused by Trump during Covid-19, the explanations and conclusions hinge on the connection between having a high faith in Trump and scoring highly on "binding" moral foundations. Psychological causation is given explanatory precedence over the social discourse that Trump espoused, and over the sociocultural underpinnings that allowed his often racist appeals to be effective.

Interestingly, assuming a different tack Cherry et al. (2021) found that displaying pro-masking messages from Trump was able to increase the likelihood of his supporters wearing a mask, suggesting a social influence beyond moral foundations. This also highlights a significant point about the interactional influence of others in masking behaviours, with such interactional influence assuming a subordinate role on MFT. As discussed, studies have illuminated the interactional influences on decisions to mask, with things like saturation of others wearing masks and others donning and removing their masks influencing people's masking behaviours (Rieger, 2020; Bokemper et al., 2021; Dillard et al., 2021; Woodcock & Schultz, 2021). Indeed, Dillard et al. (2021, p. 9) found that the influences of people not masking influenced others to also not mask, but found 'no indication that this effect was conditioned on political ideology[… which] implies an explanation that is less dependent on identity politics and more plausibly the result of the strictures of immediate social interaction'. Such points are seemingly affirmed somewhat in Bruchmann & LaPierre's (2022, p. 5) MFT-based study into Covid-19 prevention behaviours. They found that although 'binding foundations were related to reporting fewer prevention behaviors', overall their 'sample reported very high levels of prevention behaviors, which could be due to social desirability'. As well as illuminating the potential significance of intersubjective influence over moral foundations, this point also alludes to a commonly identified problem with MFT, namely, that the effects of the moral foundations often only pertain to the actions of strongly politically engaged actors (Kivikangas et al., 2021).

Applications of MFT have provided some good evidence that moral dispositions were of some significance to how people adopted and assessed masking behaviours, and that there was often some alignment between divisions in masking attitudes and political dispositions. But when taken alone, this overlooks how divisions and vocabularies of contestation were established and maintained through an amalgam of social and political discourse, as well as interactions through which standards of correct practice and phrases of moral judgement were formed and enacted. Applications of MFT often subsume the role of social interactions and discourses below the catch-all explanation that moral foundations direct our interpretations of events and information. Yet, how people interpreted their responsibility in relation to masking was clearly bound up with emerging and contested discourse and social influences as much as it was with our moral dispositions. It is not that moral dispositions are not relevant. But the explanatory power of moral dispositions (especially when framed as settled neural moral foundations) elides much of what is relevant to moral experiences of masking, including the meaningful experience of lay moralities (even if underpinned by dispositions) and how these were translated into practice, and how moral practices and modes of judgement around masking developed and were enacted in interaction (as illuminated in Chap. 3). Indeed, when it comes to explaining how the kind of interactional order practices around masking developed and drove social behaviours around masking, MFT tells us little.

Conclusion

Dominant accounts of masking given in the social sciences have often reduced people's moral positions, experiences, and practices as being the straightforward outcome of institutional imposition or pre-moulded moral foundations. As a result, they mostly overlook how a great many people came to assume meaningful senses of moral concern towards the pandemic, how such positions fed into the development of masking practices, and how these moralised positions were formed and (re)considered through interactions and in relation to the development of new interactional norms and unfolding social discourse. People arrived at moral positions, judged the behaviour of others and evaluated what should be done in normative terms, thought about how they should act, and enacted their positions through mask wearing (or otherwise). Masking became part of many people's ordinary moralities. But rather than stemming simply from either authoritative mandate or prewired moral foundations, people's ordinary moralities are composed of an amalgam of obligated or semi-obligated stipulations, interactional orders of conduct, feelings of moral responsibility, evaluations of what the right thing to do entails, senses of care, blame, judgement, and intersubjective influence (Keane, 2010; Ekberg et al., 2021).

Understanding how and why people took up and dismissed masking practices during the pandemic requires recognition that people's masking practices, the way they were influenced by others personally and politically, and how people came to disagree, were situated by a complex mixture of political and personal dispositions, responsibilities, shifting scientific guidance and political discourses, new interactional norms, senses of care and personal responsibility in the face of the pandemic, and the material and spatial domains in which they took place. Understanding this requires attention not only to changing scientific narratives and government regulations, but also consideration of how such knowledge and rules are interpreted and imperfectly translated into interactions, with these interactions sustaining people's senses and displays of what right moral behaviour in the everyday life of the pandemic entailed. It was at the level of the everyday that lay moralities towards masking were experienced, and at the level of interactions (with other people as well as other nonhuman things) that the contours of the moral practices, modes of judgement, ambiguities, and contestations of masking emerged. A focus on mask wearing in terms of everyday moral experience and practice illustrates the far from straightforward relationship that exists between authority or neural moral dispositions on the one hand, and moral practices and lay moralities on the other. Without attention to everyday interaction, the picture of the moral experience and practising of masking is lost.

References

A grim calculus: The stark choices between life, death and the economy. Apr 4th 2020. (2020). *The Economist.* Retrieved March 13, 2023, from https://www.economist.com/weeklyedition/2020-04-04

Abbott, O. (2020). *The self, relational sociology, and morality in practice.* Palgrave Macmillan.

Altman, M. C. (2022). Kant in the time of covid. *Kantian Journal, 41*(1), 89–117.

Balmer, A., Meckin, R., & Abbott, O. (2021). The temporal uses of moral things: Manifesting, anchoring and conserving caring relations within the sensorium. *Sociology, 55*(3), 619–640.

Banerjee, S., Savani, M., & Shreedhar, G. (2021). Public support for "soft" versus "hard" public policies: Review of the evidence. *Journal of Behavioral Public Administration, 4*(2).

Benhabib, S. (1992). *Situating the self: Gender, community and postmodernism in contemporary ethics.* Polity Press.

Betsch, C., Korn, L., Sprengholz, P., Felgendreff, L., Eitze, S., Schmid, P., & Böhm, R. (2020). Social and behavioral consequences of mask policies during the COVID-19 pandemic. *Proceedings of the National Academy of Sciences, 117*(36), 21851–21853.

Blum, L. (2013). Political identity and moral education: A response to Jonathan Haidt's the righteous mind. *Journal of Moral Education, 42*(3), 298–315.

Bokemper, S. E., Cucciniello, M., Rotesi, T., Pin, P., Malik, A. A., Willebrand, K., Paintsil, E. E., Omer, S. B., Huber, G. A., & Melegaro, A. (2021). Experimental evidence that changing beliefs about mask efficacy and social norms increase mask wearing for COVID-19 risk reduction: Results from the United States and Italy. *PLoS One, 16*(10), e0258282.

Bos, B., Drupp, M. A., Meya, J. N., & Quaas, M. F. (2020). Moral suasion and the private provision of public goods: Evidence from the COVID-19 pandemic. *Environmental and Resource Economics, 76*(4), 1117–1138.

Bruchmann, K., & LaPierre, L. (2022). Moral foundations predict perceptions of moral permissibility of COVID-19 public health guideline violations in United States university students. *Frontiers in Psychology, 12.*

Burr, J. (2009). Exploring reflective subjectivity through the construction of the 'ethical other' in interview transcripts. *Sociology, 43*(2), 323–339.

Carlsen, H. B., Toubøl, J., & Brincker, B. (2021). On solidarity and volunteering during the COVID-19 crisis in Denmark: The impact of social networks and social media groups on the distribution of support. *European Societies, 23*(sup1), S122–S140.

CBS News. (2020). *Exhausted doctors and nurses post images of their bruised faces after long shifts wearing protective gear.* Retrieved June 13, 2023, from https://www.cbsnews.com/news/coronavirus-health-care-bruised-faces-masks-ppe-hospitals-doctors-nurses-italy-new-york/

Chan, E. Y. (2021). Moral foundations underlying behavioral compliance during the COVID-19 pandemic. *Personality and Individual Differences, 171*, 110463.

Cheng, K.K., Lam, T.H., & Leung, C.C. (2020). Wearing face masks in the community during the COVID-19 pandemic: Altruism and solidarity. *The Lancet, 0*(0). https://doi.org/10.1016/S0140-6736(20)30918-1.

Cherry, T. L., James, A. G., & Murphy, J. (2021). The impact of public health messaging and personal experience on the acceptance of mask wearing during the COVID-19 pandemic. *Journal of Economic Behavior & Organization, 187*, 415–430.

Cornelius, T., Duran, A. T., Diaz, F., Bramley, S., Shaw, K., Schwartz, J. E., Edmondson, D., Shechter, A., & Abdalla, M. (2021). The association of transmission concerns and social distance from loved ones with distress in medical professionals providing care during the COVID-19 pandemic in new York City. *Families, Systems & Health, 39*, 499–504.

DeNora, T. (2014). *Making sense of reality: Culture and perception in everyday life.* 55 City Road.

Díaz, R., & Cova, F. (2021). Reactance, morality, and disgust: The relationship between affective dispositions and compliance with official health recommendations during the COVID-19 pandemic. *Cognition and Emotion, 0*(0), 1–17.

Dillard, J. P., Tian, X., Cruz, S. M., Smith, R. A., & Shen, L. (2021). Persuasive messages, social norms, and reactance: A study of masking behavior during a COVID-19 campus health campaign. *Health Communication, 0*(0), 1–11.

Ekberg, K., Ekberg, S., Weinglass, L., & Danby, S. (2021). Pandemic morality-in-action: Accounting for social action during the COVID-19 pandemic. *Discourse & Society, 32*(6), 666–688.

Ekici, H., Yücel, E., & Cesur, S. (2021). Deciding between moral priorities and COVID-19 avoiding behaviors: A moral foundations vignette study. *Current Psychology, 42*, 5922–5938.

Emirbayer, M., & Maynard, D. W. (2010). Pragmatism and ethnomethodology. *Qualitative Sociology, 34*(1), 221–261.

Ferguson, D. (2020, August 1). Mask rage: "One man told me I shouldn't be allowed out if I can't wear one". *The Observer.* Retrieved March 30,2023, from https://www.theguardian.com/world/2020/aug/01/mask-face-coverings-i-cant-wear-one-health-reasons

Foucault, M. (2020). *Power: The essential works of Michel Foucault 1954–1984.* Penguin.

Frega, R. (2015). The normative structure of the ordinary. *European Journal of Pragmatism and American Philosophy, VII.* https://doi.org/10.4000/ejpap.370

Gilman, L. (2022). The "selfish element": How sperm and egg donors construct plausibly moral accounts of the decision to donate. *Sociology, 56*(2), 227–243.

Glasdam, S., Sandberg, H., Stjernswärd, S., Jacobsen, F. F., Grønning, A. H., & Hybholt, L. (2022). Nurses' use of social media during the COVID-19 pandemic—A scoping review. *PLoS One, 17*(2), e0263502.

GOV.UK. (2022). *The R value and growth rate, GOV.UK.* Retrieved June 9, 2023, from https://www.gov.uk/guidance/the-r-value-and-growth-rate

Graham, A., Cullen, F. T., Pickett, J. T., Jonson, C. L., Haner, M., & Sloan, M. M. (2020). Faith in trump, moral foundations, and social distancing Defiance during the coronavirus pandemic. *Socius, 6.*

Grauel, J. (2016). Being authentic or being responsible? Food consumption, morality and the presentation of self. *Journal of Consumer Culture, 16*(3), 852–869.

Haidt, J. (2001). The emotional dog and its rational tail: A social intuitionist approach to moral judgment. *Psychological Review, 108*(4), 814–834.

Haidt, J. (2013). *The righteous mind: Why good people are divided by politics and religion* (1st ed.). Penguin.

Haidt, J., & Graham, J. (2009). Planet of the Durkheimians, where community, authority, and sacredness are foundations of morality. In J. T. Jost, A. C. Kay, & H. Thorisdottir (Eds.), *Social and psychological bases of ideology and system justification*. Oxford University Press.

Haischer, M. H., Beilfuss, R., Hart, M. R., Opielinski, L., Wrucke, D., Zirgaitis, G., Uhrich, T. D., & Hunter, S. K. (2020). Who is wearing a mask? Gender-, age-, and location-related differences during the COVID-19 pandemic. *PLoS One, 15*(10), e0240785.

Hanna, E., Martin, G., Campbell, A., Connolly, P., Fearon, K., & Markham, S. (2022). Experiences of face mask use during the COVID-19 pandemic: A qualitative study. *Sociology of Health & Illness, 44*(9), 1481–1499.

Hannah, M. G., Hutta, J. S., & Schemann, C. (2020). Thinking through Covid-19 responses with Foucault—An initial overview. *Antipode Online*. Retrieved July 1, 2021, from https://antipodeonline.org/2020/05/05/thinking-through-covid-19-responses-with-foucault/

Harper, C. A., & Rhodes, D. (2021). Reanalysing the factor structure of the moral foundations questionnaire. *British Journal of Social Psychology, 60*(4), 1303–1329.

Heine, F., & Wolters, E. (2021). Using moral foundations in government communication to reduce vaccine hesitancy. *PLoS One, 16*(11), e0259435.

Hellmann, D. M., Dorrough, A. R., & Glöckner, A. (2021). Prosocial behavior during the COVID-19 pandemic in Germany. The role of responsibility and vulnerability. *Heliyon, 7*(9), e08041.

Heritage, J., & Lindstrom, A. (1998). Motherhood, medicine, and morality: Scenes from a medical encounter. *Research on Language and Social Interaction, 31*(3–4), 397–438.

Ignatow, G. (2009). Why the sociology of morality needs Bourdieu's habitus. *Sociological Inquiry, 79*(1), 98–114.

Ji, P. (2020). Masking morality in the making: How China's anti-epidemic promotional videos present facemask as a techno-moral mediator. *Social Semiotics, 0*(0), 1–8.

Keane, W. (2010). Minds, surfaces, and reasons in the anthropology of ethics. In M. Lambek (Ed.), *Ordinary ethics: Anthropology, language, and action* (pp. 64–83). Fordham University Press.

Kim, E.-S., & Chung, J.-B. (2021). Korean mothers' morality in the wake of COVID-19 contact-tracing surveillance. *Social Science & Medicine, 270*, 113673.

Kim, J. K., & Crimmins, E. M. (2020). How does age affect personal and social reactions to COVID-19: Results from the national understanding America study. *PLoS One, 15*(11), e0241950.

Kivikangas, J. M., Fernández-Castilla, B., Järvelä, S., Ravaja, N., & Lönnqvist, J. E. (2021). Moral foundations and political orientation: Systematic review and meta-analysis. *Psychological Bulletin, 147*(1), 55–94.

Lupton, D., Southerton, C., Clark, M., & Watson, A. (2021). *The face mask in COVID times: A Sociomaterial analysis, the face mask in COVID times.* De Gruyter.

Lydall, R. (2021). *Londoners urged to wear masks on Tube and buses to avoid virus surge, Evening Standard.* Retrieved June 14, 2023, from https://www.standard.co.uk/news/london/covid-winter-surge-face-masks-public-transport-intensive-care-sadiq-khan-b970418.html

Martinelli, L., Kopilaš, V., Vidmar, M., Heavin, C., Machado, H., Todorović, Z., Buzas, N., Pot, M., Prainsack, B., & Gajović, S. (2021). Face masks during the COVID-19 pandemic: A simple protection tool with many meanings. *Frontiers in Public Health, 8*, 606635.

May, V. (2013). *Connecting self to society: Belonging in a changing world* (2013 ed.). Palgrave.

Mills, C. W. (1940). Situated actions and vocabularies of motive. *American Sociological Review, 5*(6), 904–913.

Mollborn, S., Mercer, K. H., & Edwards-Capen, T. (2021). "Everything is connected": Health lifestyles and teenagers' social distancing Behaviors in the COVID-19 pandemic. *Sociological Perspectives, 64*(5), 920–938.

Morgan, M. (2014). The poverty of (moral) philosophy: Towards an empirical and pragmatic ethics. *European Journal of Social Theory, 17*(2), 129–146.

Muqsith, M. A., Pratomo, R. R., Kuswanti, A., & Muzykant, V. L. (2021). Social solidarity movement to prevent the spread of COVID-19 pandemic in Indonesia. *Masyarakat, Kebudayaan dan Politik, 34*(2), 147–158.

Nan, X., Wang, Y., Thier, K., Adebamowo, C., Quinn, S., & Ntiri, S. (2022). Moral foundations predict COVID-19 vaccine hesitancy: Evidence from a National Survey of black Americans. *Journal of Health Communication, 27*(11–12), 801–811.

O'Farrell, C. (2020). Lock down and punish. *Foucault News.* Retrieved July 1, 2021, from https://michel-foucault.com/2020/07/25/lock-down-and-punish-2020/

Office for National Statistics. (2021). *Two-thirds of adults still plan to wear masks in shops and on public transport—Office for National Statistics.* Retrieved March 15, 2023, from https://www.ons.gov.uk/peoplepopulationandcommunity/

healthandsocialcare/healthandwellbeing/articles/twothirdsofadultsstillplantowearmasksinshopsandonpublictransport/2021-07-16

Oosterhoff, B., Palmer, C. A., Wilson, J., & Shook, N. (2020). Adolescents' motivations to engage in social distancing during the COVID-19 pandemic: Associations with mental and social health. *Journal of Adolescent Health, 67*(2), 179–185.

Pasion, R., Paiva, T. O., Fernandes, C., & Barbosa, F. (2020). The age effect on protective Behaviors during the COVID-19 outbreak: Sociodemographic, perceptions and psychological accounts. *Frontiers in Psychology, 11.*

Qian, K., & Yahara, T. (2020). Mentality and behavior in COVID-19 emergency status in Japan: Influence of personality, morality and ideology. *PLoS One, 15*(7), e0235883.

Rieger, M. O. (2020). To wear or not to wear? Factors influencing wearing face masks in Germany during the COVID-19 pandemic. *Social Health and Behavior, 3*(2), 50.

Rogers, S., et al. (2020). *How can I ask my friends to wear masks? Talking to friends, family, kids, and coworkers about COVID-19 safety | Johns Hopkins | Bloomberg School of Public Health.* Retrieved June 9, 2023, from https://publichealth.jhu.edu/2020/how-can-i-ask-my-friends-to-wear-masks-talking-to-friends-family-kids-and-coworkers-about-covid-19-safety

Sahin, O., & Ianosev, B. (2021). UK: Between managed moderation and far-right conspiracy theories. In G. Bobba & N. Hubé (Eds.), *Populism and the politicization of the COVID-19 crisis in Europe* (pp. 17–30). Springer International Publishing.

Sayer, A. (2011). *Why things matter to people: Social science, values and ethical life.* Cambridge University Press.

Scambler, G. (2020). Covid-19 as a "breaching experiment": Exposing the fractured society. *Health Sociology Review, 29*(2), 140–148.

Sin, N. L., Klaiber, P., Wen, J. H., & DeLongis, A. (2021). Helping amid the pandemic: Daily affective and social implications of COVID-19-related prosocial activities. *The Gerontologist, 61*(1), 59–70.

Sitrin, M., & Colectiva Sembrar (Eds.). (2020). *Pandemic solidarity: Mutual aid during the Covid-19 crisis.* Pluto Press.

Sotiris, P. (2020). Thinking beyond the lockdown: On the possibility of a democratic biopolitics. *Historical Materialism, 28*(3), 3–38.

Southerton, D. (2003). 'Squeezing Time': Allocating practices, coordinating networks and scheduling society. *Time & Society, 12*(1), 5–25. https://doi.org/10.1177/0961463X03012001001.

Sylvia, J. J. (2020). The biopolitics of social distancing. *Social Media + Society, 6*(3), 2056305120947661.

Tarry, H., Vézina, V., Bailey, J., & Lopes, L. (2022). Political orientation, moral foundations, and COVID-19 social distancing. *PLoS One, 17*(6), e0267136.

The Royal Society. (2020). *Face masks and coverings for the general public: Behavioural knowledge, effectiveness of cloth coverings and public messaging*. The Royal Society.

Twamley, K., Faircloth, C., & Iqbal, H. (2022). COVID labour: Making a "livable" life under lockdown. *The Sociological Review, 71*, 85–104. https://doi.org/10.1177/00380261221138203

Vartanova, I., Eriksson, K., Kirgil, Z. M., & Strimling, P. (2021). The advent of the COVID-19 epidemic did not affect Americans' endorsement of moral foundations. *Frontiers in Psychology, 12.*

Verbeek, P.-P. (2008). Obstetric ultrasound and the technological mediation of morality: A Postphenomenological analysis. *Human Studies, 31*(1), 11–26.

Vinay, R., Baumann, H., & Biller-Andorno, N. (2021). Ethics of ICU triage during COVID-19. *British Medical Bulletin, 138*(1), 5–15.

Voelkel, J.G. and Brandt, M.J. (2019) 'The effect of ideological identification on the endorsement of moral values depends on the target group', Personality and Social Psychology Bulletin, 45(6), pp. 851–863. A.

Wang, X. (2022). The role of moral foundations and attitudinal motivations in the Chinese's support for China's vaccine diplomacy during the COVID-19 pandemic. *Journal of Current Chinese Affairs*, 18681026221135096.

Warnock-Parkes, E., Thew, G. R., & Clark, D. M. (2021). Belief in protecting others and social perceptions of face mask wearing were associated with frequent mask use in the early stages of the COVID pandemic in the UK. *Frontiers in Psychology, 12.*

Wider, W., Lim, M. X., Wong, L. S., Chan, C. K., & Maidin, S. S. (2022). Should I help? Prosocial behaviour during the COVID-19 pandemic. *International Journal of Environmental Research and Public Health, 19*(23), 16084.

Woodcock, A., & Schultz, P. W. (2021). The role of conformity in mask-wearing during COVID-19. *PLoS One, 16*(12), e0261321.

Wu, Y. (2020). Witnessing the pandemic with Foucault: Power, politics, and COVID-19. *Canadian Social Science, 16*(8), 36–40.

YouGov. (2021). *People support masks, so why aren't they wearing them? | YouGov.* Retrieved March 15, 2023, from https://yougov.co.uk/topics/health/articles-reports/2021/11/09/people-support-masks-so-why-arent-they-wearing-the

Zhou, A., Liu, W., Kim, H. M., Lee, E., Shin, J., Zhang, Y., Huang-Isherwood, K. M., Dong, C., & Yang, A. (2022). Moral foundations, ideological divide, and public engagement with U.S. government agencies' COVID-19 vaccine communication on social media. *Mass Communication and Society, 0*(0), 1–26.

CHAPTER 5

Conclusion: Masks and Uncertainty

Abstract In the 1990s and early 2000s, it became common for sociologists to diagnose uncertainty and flux as the defining feature of the social world. It was claimed the contemporary world is now in a perpetual state of 'radical uncertainty', in a constant state of flux caused by old certainties being undermined by 'detraditionalization', as the relentless globalising, communicative, culturally shrinking features of late capitalism resulted in the ongoing 'negotiation' and renegotiation of practices and values previously assured by the binds of tradition. Contemporary social life was thus declared to be 'under a condition of uncertainty which is permanent and irreducible'.

Keywords Masks • Uncertainty • Practice • Interaction • Materiality • Morality

In the 1990s and early 2000s, it became common for sociologists to diagnose uncertainty and flux as the defining feature of the social world. It was claimed the contemporary world is now in a perpetual state of 'radical uncertainty' (Bauman, 1997, p. 24), in a constant state of flux caused by old certainties being undermined by 'detraditionalization' (Giddens,

O. Abbott et al., *Masking in the Pandemic*, Consumption and Public Life, https://doi.org/10.1007/978-3-031-45781-4_5

1994, p. 117), as the relentless globalising, communicative, culturally shrinking features of late capitalism resulted in the ongoing 'negotiation' and renegotiation of practices and values previously assured by the binds of tradition (Beck & Beck-Gernsheim, 2004, p. 500). Contemporary social life was thus declared to be 'under a condition of uncertainty which is permanent and irreducible' (Bauman, 1997, p. 21).

Such diagnoses of the uncertainty of society at large have somewhat gone out of fashion, especially in light of various sociological reminders that the social world has always been uncertain (Atkinson, 2008), and also that renegotiating the parameters of our social existence may be possible only in a limited fashion, even within more privileged social spheres (May & Nordqvist, 2019). That we have now lived through a period of actual extreme uncertainty sheds further doubt on theoretical claims of radical uncertainty lodged by sociologists. Not least, in a period that is referred to as "post-Covid" or "living with Covid", the thing that is perhaps most remarkable is how the social world as it was known has been able to mostly survive such a drastic and protracted rupture. In many respects, it seems that it was not perennial uncertainty that won out, but rather the pervasive drive to return to the status quo. Many things have changed. But many things that came to feel normal at the very particular time of the pandemic have already (around three years on from the onset of the pandemic as this book is being written) faded into memory.[1] Indeed, something that surprised us as authors of a book on masking is how quickly masking practices have receded (in the UK and in many other countries) from being an ordinary feature of public life to being something that is rarely seen.

This "return to normal", as it was often phrased, represents a marked shift from life during the height of the Covid-19 pandemic, in which uncertainty and flux were central. From the outset, the pandemic was characterised by uncertainties about the virus, how it should be responded to, how long it would last, and how lives would be led under the strange new circumstances engendered by Covid-related restrictions. Infection rates rose and fell in waves as new variants emerged, leading to pandemic restrictions (including mask mandates) being implemented, lifted, then implemented again. The result was that any sense of a "new normal" that had been gained was repeatedly unsettled. Masking, rates of which also fluctuated continually, was one visible expression of this ebb and flow of the pandemic. In line with this general experience of the pandemic, writing this book has itself been an exercise in uncertainty.

[1] We are of course wary of making any firm claims of being "out of the woods" or a return to normal.

Masking in the Pandemic began in 2020 as conversations and then as shared written observations between colleagues hoping to achieve little more than social and intellectual stimulation during a time of tumultuous and almost unimaginable social upheaval. We started meeting (remotely) to discuss how we, as sociologists of the everyday, should think about a social world in which the everyday had become utterly different. Our conversations turned to face masks at a time when masking was proliferating in social life, but there was still considerable ambiguity about how useful masking was in protecting people against the Covid-19 virus and whether it should be recommended on account of limited stocks of PPE. When we first discussed developing our ideas and texts into a book in 2021, masking had become a routine feature of public interactions, and it seemed that masking might be more of a perennial feature of post-pandemic life than it has proven to be. Even as we first pitched this book to Palgrave in January 2022, it felt like a brief and partial respite from the pandemic was being rapidly swept away by a wave of the Omicron variant. The universities at which we worked were holding their breath to see if we would have another severely disrupted semester of hybrid or fully online teaching. This book would have looked very different had it been published in early 2022. The key points about what masking tells us about interaction, moral and material practices, and the translation of shifting and politicised scientific discourse into action would likely have been similar to those we have made in the preceding chapters. But the general overtones of the ongoing role of masking in people's daily lives that were part of our original book proposal turned out to have a short shelf life. And this is telling of the momentous changes and turbulence that we have lived through since 2020, the period in which this book was thought of, drafted, and redrafted.

The period on which this book focuses is of course not the end of a social life of facemasks in the UK or elsewhere. Although in the UK instances of masking are (in 2023) rare, the residue of masking remains. Instructions to wear a mask in doctor surgeries continue to be visible, even if they go unheeded. Breakouts of Covid-19 infections in hospitals and care facilities that lead to masks being (re)stipulated for visitors serve as resonant reminders of what was and what might be. With threats of further overwhelming waves of Covid-19 or new pandemic outbreaks remaining high, the "afterlives" of masks lingering in cupboards and draws (discussed in Chap. 2) may well be given new life.

Much remains to be seen. But during the period focused on in this book, masking became a profoundly interesting object of pandemic sociality, which brought with it various affordances, disruptions, ambiguities, and engendered new interactional norms, moral practices, and modes of judgement. Our various areas of expertise led us to think through how the multiple dimensions of the social significance of masking connect. We have thus approached this book through three facets: materiality, relations in public, and morality. This is not to imply that these facets are in any way exhaustive of the multifaceted significance of masking to everyday social life. On the contrary, the intention throughout this book has been to explore three important facets in depth, while at the same time illuminating the integral connections that exist between these facets and to do so in a way that speaks to how social phenomena can be understood generally. As Mason (2006, p. 10) argues, 'social experience and lived realities are multi-dimensional and [...] our understandings are impoverished and may be inadequate if we view these phenomena only along a single dimension'. Our exploration of masking through its material, interactional, and moral dimensions illuminate the entwinement of social meanings and practices with the material world.

As set out in Chap. 2, face masks during the pandemic became a particularly interesting sociological object because they are, at base, a medical material thing that (after a great deal of scientific debate) offered some protection to the hitherto unknown and seemingly unassailable threat of Covid-19. As such, they became an object of intense scientific focus to assess if, when, and how masks should be worn and what contribution they can make to stemming the tide of Covid-19 while facilitating some degree of social normalcy. With claims of governments to be "following the science", masking consequently developed a strong currency in social discourse, meaning masking policies and practices became an integral medium through which the effectiveness of government responses to Covid-19 were judged by experts and laypeople alike. Masks as a material defence against Covid-19 meant they were implicitly associated with bodily vulnerabilities and the deadliness of the virus. Worn tightly across the nose and mouth, they acted as a reminder of the danger at hand, whilst yielding a physical sensation that was hard to get used to. The material features of masks were themselves subject to technical debate of what kind of masks were effective and which were not, which was then translated into interpretations at an everyday level of the kind of masks that were appropriate for certain situations. As well as choice according to comfort and protectiveness, the mask as a part of public life meant choice of style and fabric became for many a way of expressing identity (Van Gorp, 2021).

Having initially signalled the potentially infectious status of a person, as a wearable means of mitigating the risks of returning to public life after lockdown, masks became both a practical and symbolic feature of pandemic sociality. Alongside other measures, the materiality of masks allowed them to act as a facilitator of social life and interactions within it. But unlike with vaccines or recommendations about social distancing, the tangibility of masks allowed them to proliferate as an interactional norm with their own constituent practices of judgement, correction, challenge, and negotiation. As discussed in Chap. 3, masking thus made visible the establishment of a new interaction order that developed out of the rapid and intensely felt changes to relations in public wrought by the pandemic and its associated restrictions. The fluctuations in Covid-19 rates and the constantly shifting landscape of (often unclear, sometimes nonsensical) pandemic restrictions meant that social interactions in public spaces never fully settled into a "new normal" but were instead subject to ongoing uncertainty and ambiguity. This brought to light in a heightened fashion the significance of disruption for social order. In addition, while writing about face masks and how these changed the nature of public sociability, we became aware of the cultural assumptions about the significance of the 'face' that underpin much Euro-American theorisation of face-to-face encounters. These assumptions are visible for example in the rather narrow research foci related to masked interactions during the pandemic, such as emotion recognition and the ability to read facial expressions. In contrast, analysing masking practices through a critical lens means attending to the fact that a mask is not just a piece of cloth that covers half the face, but a social tool that during the pandemic amplified existing inequalities and prejudices. People's choice to mask (or not) had variable consequences depending on their social position, making public spaces even less hospitable for already racialised and marginalised groups.

The connection masking has with protection from a deadly virus and the relative ease with which it could be utilised by ordinary people in social life meant masking became not just a mundane practice, but one imbued with moral meaning and carried into interaction as a part of moral practice. Goffman argued that there is a moral order to interactional norms. As with masks, there were "correct" ways of moral performance, of comporting oneself to rules and to others through masking, and of showing one's moral rectitude by indicating awareness of rules, accounting for conduct, and appraising others. But, as argued in Chap. 4, due to the association of masking with the pandemic and with the health of others, and also the subsequent politicisation of the practice, masking carried a moral significance beyond adherence to the interaction order. Masks became a thing around which lay moralities were constructed and enacted. Masking came to be seen as the "right thing to do" by many, used to symbolise care in the face of the pandemic, to represent oneself as a responsible person, or simply to appropriately enact what was taken to be right. They became objects through which moral judgements were made and felt, sometimes unjustly. Masks became particularly emblematic of political contestation, with the materiality of masks allowing them to signify one's moralised position towards pandemic restrictions. While moralised positions were formed around many aspects of the pandemic and associated restrictions, the materiality of masks afforded them a particular role as something that can be participated in by ordinary people in social life in response to the virus. It thus became a thing of interactional moral practice and display with its own orders of practice, and a tangible object about which moral attitudes could be taken and judged.

Needless to say, the social changes wrought by the pandemic were wider ranging than what we have been able to discuss in this book. For example, in the UK and elsewhere, a huge number of people were furloughed or found themselves without a job (Wels et al., 2022), and the pandemic engendered significant and lasting changes to the ways in which many people work and study (Deole et al., 2023). But what is unique about masking, and why we chose to focus on it, is that it gave sociologists a perhaps unparalleled opportunity to observe the rise and fall of a new interactional and moral practice as it happened before our eyes. Whereas social change and the development of interactional and moral practices is generally thought of as something that happens gradually, masking rapidly became a particularly visible means through which everyday lives were lived and made possible in the pandemic. Masks were part of what was for a time a "new normal" that people were trying to get used to or resisting. What is interesting, and what we have attempted to observe throughout this book, is how quickly and seemingly spontaneously new practices, modes of judgement, and moralised positions sprung up, often in ways that went beyond the stipulations of official guidance. The materiality of masks was integral to this as a visible marker and a medicalised thing, but also as an object through which sense-making could be channelled at a time of profound uncertainty, as discussed in Chap. 2.

In contrast to Latour's (1990) view of technology as a crystallisation of society, a focus on masking shows that social processes perform a capacity to buffer material and political change. Masks, as a visible object, are probably best not thought of as a singular practice of "masking". Instead, they are a common material object enrolled in many different practices and processes of solidarity, morality, interaction, fashion, health, and so on (see Hand & Shove, 2007). It seems that how aspects of these masking practices developed (e.g. how people interpreted the material sensations of masking, experienced public space in relation to masked or unmasked others, and how people produced ethical judgments and lay moralities around masks) depended on established social orderings (and disruptions within these) through which changes associated with the pandemic and masking were incorporated. For instance, the ways that people previously unaccustomed to being publicly "noticed" and who felt unusually conspicuous in terms of masking (Chap. 3), depends on social processes of identifying bodies, judging them, and making them feel and experience particular sensations. It is in such social processes that some uncertainties were dealt with in ways that incorporate new material assemblages of humans and masks.

Our final point, then, is that masking offers a unique lens through which to study the role of everyday interactions in sense-making during periods of uncertainty. But the interactionist stance we have largely followed throughout this book offers a view of uncertainty that contrasts with the grand theoretical diagnosis of a new age of perennial, unresolvable uncertainty offered by theorists in the 1990s and the early 2000s. Interactionist sociologists argue uncertainty is (and always has been) a common feature of interactions, and it is (to a significant degree) through participation in social practices that uncertainties in interactions are worked through (Emirbayer & Maynard, 2010). Such perspectives emphasise how indeterminacy is resolved through 'the continual active work of social ordering and sense producing' that people engage in 'to coordinate social relations' (Bottero, 2019, p. 177).

These points developed a new force during a time when uncertainty and ambiguity in social life achieved a new zenith. The social life of face masks in the pandemic was fundamentally implicated with uncertainties over material effectiveness and appropriate usage, ambiguities in stipulated rules, the negotiation of these rules into practice, and indeterminacy yielded by varying levels of acceptance and diligence. Masks thus became objects, prominent through their visibility, through which sense-making was channelled to resolve new and ever-shifting uncertainties that characterised everyday life in the pandemic. And it was through interaction in everyday life that orders and modes of practice beyond stipulated rules were established and negotiated in the pursuit of intelligibility, assurance, and stability. Indeed, as discussed in Chap. 3, the kind of disruptions produced by such uncertainty were integral to this process. This alludes to how complex social arrangements, even in the most challenging circumstances, are made manifest through social activity (Hughes & Sharrock, 2007). It also shows that even in the most profound times of uncertainty, sense continues to be made through interactions. But we argue that explaining how social activity produced the masking practices that for a brief while framed everyday interactions requires understanding masking across its material, interactional, and moral dimensions. And likewise, the material, the interactional, or the moral dimensions of masking in the pandemic are not explicable without each other, and none of them on their own is sufficient if we are to gain a coherent understanding of how masking contributed to, and was an expression of, the ever-shifting terrain of social life.

References

Atkinson, W. (2008). Not all that was solid has melted into air (or liquid): A critique of Bauman on individualization and class in liquid modernity. *The Sociological Review, 56*(1), 1–17.

Bauman, Z. (1997). *Postmodernity and its discontents.* Polity.

Beck, U., & Beck-Gernsheim, E. (2004). Families in a runaway world. In J. Scott, J. Treas, & M. Richards (Eds.), *The Blackwell companion to the sociology of families* (pp. 499–514). John Wiley & Sons, Ltd.

Bottero, W. (2019). *A sense of inequality.* Rowman and Littlefield.

Deole, S. S., Deter, M., & Huang, Y. (2023). Home sweet home: Working from home and employee performance during the COVID-19 pandemic in the UK. *Labour Economics, 80*, 102295.

Emirbayer, M., & Maynard, D. W. (2010). Pragmatism and ethnomethodology. *Qualitative Sociology, 34*(1), 221–261.

Giddens, A. (1994). *Beyond left and right: The future of radical politics.* Stanford University Press.

Hand, M., & Shove, E. (2007). Condensing practices: Ways of living with a freezer. *Journal of Consumer Culture, 7*(1), 79–104.

Hughes, J., & Sharrock, W. (2007). *Theory and methods in sociology: An introduction to sociological thinking and practice.* Macmillan International Higher Education.

Latour, B. (1990). Technology is society made durable. *The Sociological Review, 38*(1_suppl), 103–131.
Mason, J. (2006). Mixing methods in a qualitatively driven way. *Qualitative Research, 6*(1), 9–25.
May, V., & Nordqvist, P. (2019). *Sociology of personal life* (2nd ed., 2019 ed.). Red Globe Press.
Van Gorp, B. (2021). Face masks as floating signifiers during the COVID-19 pandemic in Belgium. *Visual Studies, 36*(2), 124–132.
Wels, J., Booth, C., Wielgoszewska, B., Green, M. J., Di Gessa, G., Huggins, C. F., Griffith, G. J., Kwong, A. S., Bowyer, R. C., Maddock, J., & Patalay, P. (2022). Mental and social wellbeing and the UK coronavirus job retention scheme: Evidence from nine longitudinal studies. *Social Science & Medicine, 308*, 115226.

Index

O. Abbott et al., *Masking in the Pandemic*, Consumption and Public Life, https://doi.org/10.1007/978-3-031-45781-4

FSC
www.fsc.org
MIX
Papier | Fördert
gute Waldnutzung
FSC® C083411

Kolibri 360 GmbH
Ferdinand-Jühlke-Straße 7
99095 Erfurt, Deutschland
produktsicherheit@kolibri360.de